FREE BORN

350 Years of Eastern Shore African American History

The Adams/Beckett Family

by

William Crawford Samuel Adams

HERITAGE BOOKS
2018

HERITAGE BOOKS
AN IMPRINT OF HERITAGE BOOKS, INC.

Books, CDs, and more—Worldwide

For our listing of thousands of titles see our website
at
www.HeritageBooks.com

Published 2018 by
HERITAGE BOOKS, INC.
Publishing Division
5810 Ruatan Street
Berwyn Heights, Md. 20740

International Standard Book Number
Paperbound: 978-0-7884-1625-5

DEDICATION

This book is dedicated to all my ancestors who endured through slavery and freedom, Black Codes and Jim Crow; and to my grandfathers and father who, by their examples, taught me the values that made their success possible.

I would also like to thank my wife, Carolyn, without whose inspiration and continued perseverance, I would not have undertaken this fascinating journey into my "roots."

FREE BORN

TABLE OF CONTENTS

FREE BORN

FREE BORN

INTRODUCTION

It was 1976 and television's first miniseries, "Roots" burst upon the American consciousness. All America became transfixed by the ground-breaking docudrama based on Alex Haley's search for his ancestors. That was also the same year I met my wife and I vividly remember watching the series together. Several years later, based on the lingering impact of the series, I decided to investigate the roots of my Adams ancestry. I had a good start because I knew there had been three generations of William Adams' before me, and they came from McDaniel in Talbot County on Maryland's Eastern Shore. I also knew that my Grandmother Adams' maiden name was Beckett and she was from Accomack on the Eastern Shore of Virginia.

But I was rather pessimistic about the chances of finding any information about any ancestors before the Civil War. I thought that maybe, if I were lucky, I would be able to trace the surname Adams back to someone who had been the slave owner. Even that seemed not too likely, but I wanted to try. I hoped I might be able to do what Alex Haley had done; but realistically I thought would probably just hit a dead-end with the slavery period.

FREE BORN

How wrong I was! Although I couldn't match Haley's success of tracing all the way back to Africa, I was able to discover a rich heritage of freedom extending back over three hundred years. The more I researched, the more I found about the fascinating life of free blacks in colonial Virginia and Maryland.

FREE BORN

THE BECKETT FAMILY

FREE BORN

BEGINNING THE SEARCH

Checking the U. S. Census records was the first step in my search. I hoped to get information on my families for the time after the Civil War until they emigrated from the Eastern Shore in the late 1890's. This began my long acquaintance with microfilm loading, rolling, scrolling and squinting.

While on a visit to Salisbury my wife, Carolyn, visited the Eastern Shore History Library at Salisbury State University, her alma mater, to see if there was any information on the Beckett family. I knew Grandmother's name was Recie Beckett and her father's name was Major Beckett. I also knew that in the late 1890s she had gone from Accomack on the Eastern Shore of Virginia, to Philadelphia, Pennsylvania, and then to Riderwood in Baltimore County.

Armed with this information my wife checked the Accomack County, Virginia Census records that were on microfilm. On the 1900 census she found Major Beckett listed along with his wife, Jane, and children Annie, Lottie and Ed. It made sense that Grandmother Recie was not on that census, as she had already left by then.

The librarian then suggested that we contact Mary Ann Scarborough, a history professor at Salisbury State University. Ms. Scarborough told us that many family names in the area are shared by both white and black families, making research sometimes confusing. However, she then said that to her knowledge, there had never been any white Becketts. She also told us about a book entitled, Free African Americans of North Carolina and Virginia, by Paul Heinegg that included the Beckett genealogy. She volunteered to send us a copy of the information on the Becketts from the book.

I could hardly believe my eyes when I received the material. There was the ancestry of the Beckett family beginning with a slave named Peter Beckett! According to Mr. Heinegg's book, Peter Beckett was first shown on the tithable or tax list for the year 1671 in the household of John Eyre.

The book continued to trace the Beckett descendants through several generations down to the mid 1700s. To have such documented information seemed too unreal to be possible. Here was proof that the Beckett ancestors had been in America and been free- **not slaves-** for over 300 years!

The references in the book to court documents showed Becketts with wills and court cases and marriages and children and even one Beckett who was a sailor in the Virginia Navy in the Revolutionary War. Most of all, it revealed how the Becketts became free originally.

According to Mr. Heinegg's research, the slave Peter Beckett married a white indentured servant Elizabeth Kettle and had a child named Kettle Tony[1]. I could hardly believe my eyes!

By law, then, the children received the free status of the mother, so all their children were free.

That a slave had married a white indentured servant woman was too incredible. It gave me chills when I reflected on the implications of that history and our lives. Here in the late 1600s, Peter, the slave, had married a white indentured servant; and I echoed that relationship over 300 years later. It made me wonder if there were some invisible hand of fate at work that had sent me searching the past to discover this incredible coincidence.

THE GENEALOGY VACATION

The Records

I needed to see the proof of all of this by examining the court records myself. So I decided we would take a genealogy vacation. Armed with the references we had found, my wife and I set off to the Eastern Shore of Virginia and the court records at Eastville.

When we arrived at Eastville, it was easy to find the central square with the old jail, old courthouse and the current courthouse. The court clerk was glad to help and told me of many others who had done research there. She showed me the shelves with rows of huge old ledger books containing the old records of Northampton County dating back to 1632.

These records describe life at the time in a series of pen sketches, odd and interesting in quaint characters, very difficult for modern readers to understand. When you take the time you find glimpses of the real people as they lived; when they broke the Sabbath, committed fornication, spoke out in their depositions about their masters, relatives and neighbors. This was where I found over 300 years of Beckett records.

I took the first volume that had the tithable lists from the 1670s and carried it to the long, standup counter and began to turn the pages. Finally I got to the page referenced in Mr. Heinegg's book that contained the 1671 list. There was Peter Beckett listed under the household of John Eyre along with Tho: Driggeus and Mary Crew. Here was the actual record! I continued finding many of the other references and getting the clerk to make copies. These documents alone made the trip more than worthwhile.

After we left the Courthouse, we went to the library in Accomack where I found additional microfilm records census records and the 1832 List of Free Blacks. I wondered why such a special survey of free blacks had been done apart from the census records. I found that around this time whites were becoming increasingly apprehensive about the growing numbers of free blacks in their midst. In an attempt to find a solution to this problem, they funded what was called the Colonization Society. The Society's goal was to recruit and to pay for transportation of any free blacks who choose to immigrate to Liberia in Africa and the list was compiled to identify all these free blacks. There were thirty-five Becketts on that list, all with the notation "Born Free" beside their names.

I also found many other Becketts in all the census records from 1800 through 1900. I recorded all their names so that later I would be able to analyze the information later on to trace my family's links. Next I checked the courthouse in Accomack where I looked at death certificates, marriage licenses and birth registries. In that courthouse I found a surprise. There was a marriage license for a Recie I. Beckett to a Mr. Coleburn dated 1895. I had never heard that my Grandmother Recie had been married before she married my Grandfather Adams. Major and Jane Beckett were listed as her parents- so that verified it had to be my Grandmother.

Eyre Hall

Armed with all this information, we returned to the motel to begin to review and organize the materials. Before I got the chance to really start this process, we were looking at the hotel's local guidebook and saw listed an "Eyre Hall." The guidebook said this plantation home dated back to the 1700s and that its English style gardens were open year round to visitors.

So we decided to go there assuming it had to be linked to the John Eyre who had owned Peter Beckett. As I drove up the long driveway past seemingly unending flat fields towards the house, I was filled with mixtures of potent emotions. Here I was on the same grounds where I believed the Beckett ancestors had lived over 300 years ago.

In my mind's eye, I could almost see the men and women, working those very same fields tending the growing of tobacco. I looked around and I saw a group of black workers on the opposite side of the field watching us come up the drive. It was almost as though my Beckett ancestors were reaching out to me across three hundred years.

As I pulled up in front of the house a tall white-haired man casually dressed got out of a pickup truck and met me. I thought he was the caretaker, and told him that I had traced my ancestors to the Eyre Plantation. He told us to feel free to explore the gardens. The gardens were lovely - exemplifying the traditional, colonial style English boxwood garden with its geometric patterns and unique musty odor. The garden also contained the romantic crumbling remains of a colonial orangerie and several benches peacefully shaded and cozy amidst the boxwood rows.

After we had been there for a while just soaking up the feeling, the white haired gentleman came up to us and identified himself as Furlong Baldwin, the current owner of the estate. As he was showing us around the gardens, he told us that he was the descendant of John Eyre's brother Thomas Eyre. It was fascinating to realize that standing together over 300 years after the fact, were the 11th generation relatives of the slave master and the slave. In the past there had been wars, pestilence, racial strife, but at that moment we were two men of varied backgrounds who had walked different paths to meet at where it all began.

Mr. Baldwin did tell us, however, that during Peter's time, the family's land would have been located further down the peninsula, closer to the Magothy Bay. It was a little disappointing to learn that this was not the exact ground that Peter had trod, but the connections were still astounding. Later research would reveal that my ancestors did remain connected to the Eyre family until the time when they probably would have been on this very land.

When I returned home I began to put together all the puzzle pieces of the Beckett genealogy using the research and the information gained on this interesting vacation. After I began to assemble the puzzle I realized there were more questions I should have asked and avenues I should have explored. I have since learned that in genealogical research one answer usually leads to only more questions! Still I had gotten enough original documentation on which to base my family history.

VIRGINIA'S EASTERN SHORE

Virginia's Eastern Shore, a slender peninsula with a northeast- southwest trend, borders the lower Chesapeake Bay on the west, Maryland's peninsular counties on the north, and the Atlantic Ocean on the east. It is only about seventy-five miles long and six to eight miles wide, with a land area of 682 square miles, excluding coastal islands and salt marshes.

The first name of the peninsula, "Ye Plantacon of Accawmacke " came from the Indian inhabitants and meant "Over-the-water" or "on-the-other-side-of-the-water" place. In 1643 the name was changed to Northampton after Northamptonshire in England. Twenty years later the peninsula was divided into two counties and both historical names came in use, the lower portion retaining the name Northampton, and the upper portion reverting to Accomack.

It contains no major rivers but rather its bayside is heavily indented by small creeks and inlets that separate numerous necks of land. These necks and the contiguous land along the bayside of the shore are predominantly flat and less than twenty-five feet above sea level. It was on the bayside necks that the English colonists first patented large tracts of land during the seventeenth century. Proximity to navigable water for transportation of the tobacco staple was then a vital matter.

The first permanent English settler, Thomas Savage, came to the Shore about 1614, and his descendants still live there today. Other settlers followed rapidly, and a county government soon was established in 1632 with the commissioners. In 1663, following the division of the peninsula into the two counties, the first courthouse was built at the "Towne," a small settlement on the bayside between Cherrystone Inlet and Kings Creek.

They first held meetings as a court in individual members' homes and other privately owned buildings such as taverns and ordinaries, migrating from one place to another. This system was modeled on the English System. Before the Revolution, the Anglican Church (Church of England), the official or "established" church, was also a major factor in Virginia's government. Both the church and the secular government were supported by taxes levied for that purpose. Taxes in seventeenth century Virginia were assessed on people, not land or livestock. The definition of the taxable or tithable changed from time to time. But in 1620s it included "all those that worke in the grounde". The wives of the planters were excluded. It was commonly held that only "wenches" – white indentured servants of slaves- would actually cultivate tobacco.

FREE BORN

In 1645 all Negro women from the age of 16 to 60 were adjudged to be tithable.

The early court records kept by the clerks in their homes miraculously have survived to the present day and are the oldest continuous county court records in the United States, dating from 1632.

FREE BORN

INDENTURED SERVANTS

During the 1600's, there was a great urge felt by many to leave England. Much of the populace wanted to go to the New World. The motivations were many. My history books told me of those with noble reasons, those who felt compelled by their need to practice their religion in freedom, those who were adverse to the political system and its taxes, and those adventurers who dreamed of unlimited land and riches beyond their imagination. But the books did not tell me of the recruitment of labor to the American tobacco plantations, which was achieved in very large measure through the emptying of English jails, workhouses, brothels and houses of correction.

The city streets were home to many children. They were homeless waifs who were constantly dodging the authorities who threatened them with workhouses. The children preferred the streets by begging, scrounging and stealing rather than life in the workhouses. Periodically they were rounded up and put into the Bridewell Hospital. This was really a house of correction used to hold the children until they could be shipped off to the New World.

FREE BORN

Headrights

The authorities in England had chartered the Virginia Company (named after Elizabeth the Queen). The idea was to make landowners and thus taxpayers of the immigrants. They were allowed to patent fifty acres of land for each person whose passage was paid to Virginia. It made no difference whose passage was paid for or who paid it. It could be for himself, his family, his friends or relatives, his slaves or his contracted servants. The latter were most prevalent.

These people were known as headrights. The master received the right to receive (patent) fifty acres of land for each "head" whose passage he paid. Often a prosperous person could import hundreds of people and receive thousands of acres. The fare across the ocean was six pounds of English money (or 120 lbs. of tobacco) and three more for administrative expenses in England.

The master did not have to accompany or escort his headrights across the ocean. It was only necessary for him to pay the expenses to an agent who made all the arrangements. And the master could save up his headrights until he had enough to patent a large chunk of adjacent land. To accomplish this he registered them with the local courts until he was ready to make his claim. And it was these indentured servants who provided the labor to make improvements on the home and or cultivate the crops of tobacco on the land of their master thus allowing him to continue the sequence.

By the system of indentured servitude, any person over the age of fifteen could bind him or herself over to a master or shipping merchant who, in return for free passage, could quite literally sell themselves into servitude in the plantations for a period of two to seven years. Many of the servants were criminals who came to avoid jail sentences and others had been captured and transported against their will. Bristol merchants had little care as to how the servants were obtained, the trade was profitable and the merchants could afford to take them free because of the high price they would bring upon arrival in America. So a trading pattern was set for a century and a half of an outward cargo of laborers to be exchanged for a return consignment of tobacco.[2]

Life in America

The ships bound for Virginia sailed southwest to the Azores and then turned nearly due west to the Capes of Virginia. The voyages were not easy. It is estimated that in the period 1620 to 1680, some 35% of women and 50% of men sent to the Americas as indentured servants died on shipboard.[3]

Once ashore the life was no easier. They were often chained together and taken to public markets to be inspected by purchasers and then auctioned and sold to the highest bidder just like the slave markets. The difficulty of making a successful escape was overwhelming. Without formal discharge papers, any wanderer could be apprehended and questioned. The newspapers ran advertisements offering rewards for the return of runaway servants just as they did for runaway slaves. Indians were paid if they helped capture them. Attempted escape from servitude was punished ferociously. In Virginia, thirty-nine lashes of the whip were prescribed for the offense, in Maryland ten days additional service could be exacted for each day of freedom. Often iron collars and balls and chains would be used on an escaped servant just as on the escaped slave.

Though some had the good fortune to be sold to good planters many others faced a much crueler life. In most cases they were given only a bare minimum to eat. Severe punishment could be meted out and they could be given extensions to their time of servitude and "whipped and worked.". For example, in November 1665 in Accomack, Thomas Roberts courageously spoke out against the treatment of William Jones, a servant whipped by four men who took turns beating him till they could no longer stand.[4]

In another case, according to these court records, John Manington, a servant of Thomas Leatherberry, was abused by both his master and his fellow servants until he died.

Neighbors testified that they saw Leatherberry coming up the hill "driving his man before him " When asked where he was going with his man, Leatherberry replied that he had given him a drench(a purging drink often forced down the throat) and was now walking him. Later that day another servant was seen beating him with a stick. The next day Manington stumbled in front of the fireplace and fell pulling the hot kettle of wort(beer in the making) down on himself. While he was down another servant struck him with a loblolly pine stick and he never got up.[5]

If a servant turned upon his master, punishment was harsh. Hannah Snowswell after being struck by her mistress, turned on her, putting one arm around her neck and the other around her middle. For this offense she received 25 lashes "well applied to her naked shoulders" and one more year of servitude. When Major John Tilney criticized the work of Daniell Clansie, he grabbed Tilney and struck him and attempted to hit Tilney and another man with a hoe. For this he got 20 lashes.[6]

Elizabeth Spriggs wrote home to England:

> What we unfotunate English people suffer here is beyond the probability of you in England to conceive. Let it suffice that I, one of the unhappy number, am toiling almost day and night, and very often in the horses' drudgery with only this comfort that: "You

> bitch you do not half enough" and then tied up and whipped to that degree that you'd not serve an animal; scarce anything to eat but Indian corn and salt and that even begrudged. Nay many negroes arte better used; almost naked, no shoes or stockings to wear, and the comfort after slaving during Master's pleasure what rest we can get is to wrap ourselves in a blanket and lie upon the ground.[7]

No wonder that by 1671 still only one in five lived through the first year.[8] The major killers were contagious diseases, smallpox, malaria, dysentery. This mortality rate continued through the end of the century. Before 1680, the life expectancy for a migrant was only about forty years. About half the children born were dead before age 20, a quarter before age one. A majority of the marriages were broken within seven years by the death of one of the partners. In 1644 the population of the Eastern Shore was approximately 340, by 1662 it had grown to only 707.[9]

AFRICAN IMMIGRANTS

The first immigrants of African descent arrived in Virginia in August 1619. Over the next forty years Virginia's Negro population grew slowly, and at mid century it numbered only about three hundred. The first known account of Negroes on the Eastern Shore of Virginia was in the late 1620s. In

1635 the wealthy Indian trader and planter, Charles Harmar, listed eight Negroes on his claim for a large tract of land in Northampton County. Harmar died a few years later, and the slaves in his estate became the property of Nathaniel Little upon his marriage to the widow Anne Harmar. In 1640, the Littletons claimed fourteen more slaves as headrights in a joint land patent.

All available research indicates that all the Negroes who arrived in Northampton came in as slaves. Most came to Virginia from the West Indies rather than directly from Africa, as their success in dealing with planters and their apparent good health indicated that before arriving on the Eastern Shore they had acquired a knowledge of English and been exposed to New World diseases.

The appearance of many with Portuguese surnames such as Fernando, Francisco and Rodriggus suggests that the suppliers were Dutch merchants operating out of New Amsterdam (New York). The Portuguese Dutch connection went back decades and involved the Dutch seizure of major Portuguese trading posts along the coast of Angola and Zaire. These slaving stations may well have been the places from which Rodriggus and others originated. When the Dutch briefly conquered New Holland (Brazil) in the late 1630s, their interest in the slave trade expanded, and they transported thousands of Angolans to the New World. Some of these men and women eventually found their way to New Netherland and from there through trade to Virginia's Eastern Shore.[10] Historians establish the size of Northampton County's Negro population after 1660 with some certainty. The tithable list for 1664 reveals that sixty-two Negroes lived in the county, representing 14% of the total number of tithables. By 1677 these figures had risen only slightly, with 75 Negroes both slave and free making up 16% of the tithables. During the period 1664-1677 there were 1,043 names on all the surviving lists of which 101 were Negro or mulatto men and women.

At this time on the Eastern Shore of Virginia, although most Negroes and only Negroes were slaves, it does not appear that the logic of racist slavery was yet reflected in the beliefs and practices of either whites or Negroes. For a short while at least, the forces for assimilation seemed almost as strong as those that were to lead to segregation. Most Negroes had begun to learn, and in a few cases clearly mastered, the language and ways of white colonists. Negroes and whites, far from displaying mutual hostility or contempt, apparently worked together well.[11] For example, whenever slaves were caught stealing food, they usually had white confederates. When they ran away they usually did so in the company of white servants.

FREE BORN

Sexual intimacy was another product of the close relations between Negroes and lower class whites. Few white slaveholders seem to have kept Negro concubines in the colonial Chesapeake. Despite the common assumption that race mixing occurred mainly at the instigation of wealthy white male planters who imposed their will on their female slaves, this was not the origin of most mulattos and free Negroes in the Upper South. During the Colonial era most of Virginia's free Negro population were descendants from white indentured servants, women as well as men.[12]

At least five or six marriages did occur between free Negro men and free white women, and there were many other instances of slaves fathering mulatto children by white maidservants who worked on the same plantations. Until after 1680 or so, most of the free colored population on the Eastern Shore was Negro or if mulatto, the issue of lawful marriages between free Negro men and free white women. The early interracial marriages occasioned little comment, negative or positive, in the court records.[13]

Slavery to Freedom

The legal definition of mixed race children of Negroes and whites had supposedly been settled in 1662 when the Virginia legislature enacted laws prohibiting interracial marriages and declaring that the children followed the status of their mother. However, this was one of many laws passed by the Virginia legislature that the Eastern Shore ignored when desired.

Occasionally the name of a free Negro planter would simply appear in the documents, and the absence of background materials suggests that some freedom agreements were either lost or never recorded. A few Negroes seem to have gained freedom after promising to serve an especially long period of time, and for reasons that remain obscure, their masters did not demand money, tobacco or servants in exchange for liberty.[14]

During the period 1664-1677, 13 Negroes, ten men and three women were or became householders. That represented 19% (10 of 53) Negro male in Northampton were free. The 1688 tithable list alone yields an even higher percentage. In that year approximately 29 percent of the Northampton Negroes had gained freedom.[15]

The free Negroes of Northampton could never take their freedom for granted. Self-purchase, however achieved, represented only the first step on the road to becoming a free planter. Full independence demanded access to land ownership. Although there are many records of other Negroes obtaining land, I could not find any records of the Becketts ever owning any. Free Negroes also supported their families through many kinds of agricultural pursuits, with tobacco cultivation always important. Their prosperity also depended heavily upon their success in raising livestock.

After gaining their freedom the freedman apparently worked well within the existing social system. The court records show that their names appear not as anonymous tithables, but as men and women who bought property, formed families, participated in the communities and courts, and provided for their children. It appears that they did not flourish by separating themselves from the rest of the community but rather they became part of the network, and they were as successful as they could be in dealing with white planters, great and small, servants and slaves.

The Court

Beyond the family, the Northampton County Court was the central institution in the lives of all the settlers including the of the free Negro planters. At one time or another almost everyone in the county came before the court for one thing or another. At that time they still had that right and they were not treated any differently than the whites. As often as not, they initiated the proceedings, they sued their neighbors and were sued in return. On the whole their record before the county court seems neither better nor worse than that compiled by small white planters.

FREE BORN

What follows is information on a representative sampling of several of these court cases involving free blacks . The information is taken from the court records and from the books by Deal and Breen and Innes.

Anthony Longo [Witness]

In May 1641 Richard Newton, a small planter, described to the members of the county court an interracial gathering at which he had been present the previous weekend. Newton stated that "upon Sonday last...being at the home of Anthony Longo, and John Parramore and Henry Williams being there allso," a quarrel erupted between Williams and Parramore over several yards of cotton cloth.

The men seem to have been drunk. Williams demanded the material, but the other man put him off, promising delivery or suitable substitution in due time. While Newton and Longo watched in amazement, Williams hit Parramore across the face, "and not therewith content but againe stooke him, and swearing drew a punyard and sayd hee could fynd [it] in his heart to stabb the sayd Parramore."

The court ordered Williams to beg Parramore's forgiveness for the beating, especially since it had occurred on "the Saboth day," and Parramore was given ten days to produce the cotton cloth. The fact that whites had been socializing at the home of a Negro man did not strike the justices as noteworthy. On another occasion Anthony Longo's Son James took exception with a white man that owed him a days work but didn't show up as planned.

James Longo

One June day in 1687, a young man named Richard Sholster was riding with the daughter of John Wasbourne to a neighboring plantation to gather cherries. The lane passed by the fence and house of James Longo. Sholster knew he owed a day's work to Longo, but was astonished by Longo's outburst:

> Longo came running...and leaped over the fence furiously and tooke upp a corne stock in his hand and laye hold of your deponent's horse's bridle and fell a calling this deponent roque and rascal and severall other scurrilous words over and over againe threatening to beat [me] and asked mee why I did not come to paye him a dayes worke.
> I civilly answered that in expectation of a season to plant in , I did not come. Presently after hee layd his hands upon my shoulder in a violent manner, and furiously pulled mee off the horse to the ground, the force of which fall hurt my head and shoulder and caused great paine upon the same, and the girle that satt behinde mee on the said horse did vehemently cry out being frightened at his action.

Longo was fined one hundred pounds of tobacco and ordered to post bond to keep the peace in the future--a fairly mild punishment that probably would have been harsher had he assaulted someone of real standing in the community.

Philip Mongum

Another episode, in November 1687, illustrates how Negroes participated in the rowdy give and take that characterized the social life of most whites in early Northampton Virginia. One Sunday in the middle of the month, a group of white neighbors gathered at Mongun's house for some drinking and carousing. Mongum, his wife Mary, and son Philip Jr., were the only Negroes present.

Among the whites were William Cowdrey, a former ordinary keeper who had married the wealthy widow of Mongun's deceased landlord John Savage; George Corbin, a small farmer who may have also been related to the savages; William Baker and John Booker, both poor men, possibly tenant farmers like Mongun; the wives of Corbin and Booker; and several others, unnamed.

After a good deal of "drinkinge and carrousinge as well without doores as within," some of the men began quarreling with Booker. Their mood turned nasty, and Booker was severely beaten. His wife Ann, who like her husband was just over fifty, later recounted what happened:

> [The men] did drinke to a great heighth, at last all the said persons fell upon my said husband and did most cruelly beate him, my

said husband cryinge for god sake spare my life.
The said Corbett replyed thou short arse devil I will kill you immediately, for a man is noe more to me to kill in my humour then a mouse.
Old Mongum after many bad words asked his son for the sword, who answered hee could not tell but would immediately strike his heeles as high as his head, which hee imediately did.
The said old Mongum fetched out his gunn and said in [sic] please god I will kill some body imediately for I must doe it, upon which I runn away and the said Mongums son followed me and gave me severall kicks, upon which, the said Corbett said an old bitch, kick her to death.
And this examinant further saith that shee heard William Cowdrey and William Baker say kill him kill him, what you stay soe longe about him that wee may goe to drinkinge againe and made a fire to burne him and did fline him in the fire and burnt some part of him , but was ha[u]led out againe by my selfe and the old Negro. Booker's assailants were ordered to post bonds for their good behavior and pay fines of 500 pounds tobacco each.

There were a number of occasions that Negroes were used to testify in court for a fellow planter. This didn't always go well, especially if it caused an inconvenience for the witness.

FREE BORN

Anthony Longo

Neene reported his experience with Longo in these words:

> Sayth that comeinge to Tony Longo his house with a warrent of Major Walker, Your deponent asked him whether hee would goe alonge to Mr. Walkers with mee. his answere was what shall I goe to Mr. Walker for: goe about your business you idle Rascall: Upon those slightinge tearnes, I told him I had a warrant for him, sayeinge, will you go with that, hee made nee answer, shitt of your warrant have I (said hee) nothing to doe but go to Mr. Walker, go about your business you idle Rascal as did likewise his wife, with such noyse that I could hardly hear my owne words, reading the warrant to them, which when I had done reaseinge, the said Tony stroke att mee, and gave mee some blowes, soe perseavinge it was to little purpose to staye with him.
>
> I went to Mr. Littleton's house and requested David Baker to goe to Tony Longos with mee only to testifie that I had a warrant from Mr Walker for his appearance before him.
>
> Daniel Baker att my request went with mee which when wee came , I desired him to read it to him which he did, his answers were that hee would not goe, hee must gather his corne, Now it beinge about the sun settinge (or somethinge after) I told him wee might goe to night and neither hinder himselfe much, nor mee, But his answer was thats a goode one nowe. I have bine att worke shall goe to Mr. Walkers I your said deponent request him to

goe alone with mee and as I could not make my debt appear I would give him for his payment 20 lb of tobacco. Well said hee I cannot goe, why when shall I attend you said your deponent tomorrowe or next daye, or next weeake Ile goe with you att any time his answer was in generall, well, Ile goe when my corne is in --whereupon I bade him good night, and left him, and returned the warrant the next day.

FREE BORN

THE BEGINNINGS OF THE BECKETTS

The name of Beckett first appears when a John Beckett is listed along with thirty-nine others in the "headrights" granted to Col. Argoll Yardley in 1654.[16] His origin and how long he had been on the Eastern Shore are unknown.

A James Beckett then appears on the Tithable List of 1665. This is probably the same individual as the one on the headrights list. He appears on every Tithable list 1665-1674 in the household of Thomas Moore with the exception of 1671 when he is listed in the household of Thomas Poynter.[17] His name appears to be spelled at times as Bookett, Buckett, Birkett and Brackett because "in an age when not everyone could write, much less spell with uniformity, those who could write were free to make their own spelling rules based on the phonics they heard. They often did not feel a need to be consistent".[18]

The last time James Beckett's name appears is in 1675 when he is the head of his own household in John Michael's Division.[19] This indicates that he had been an indentured servant up until that time and had then attained the freedom to head his own household. The Michael's Division included the John Eyre, Thomas Moore and Thomas Poynter households all in close proximity.

In addition, John Eyre's mother, Susannah Baker, married Captain Francis Pott after Eyre's death. Pott's godson was Argoll Yardley[20] whose headrights included Beckett. In 1658 some of Pott's land was sold to Thomas Moore in whose household James Beckett appears on the tithable lists. After Pott's death Susannah married Col. William Kendall. In 1668 1,500 acres was deeded to Col Kendall "for the use of John Eyre, Thomas and Danielle Eyre".[21] In 1670 as the Eyre boys had now become of age, the patent was reissued directly to them jointly. John received 533 acres above the lower part of Thomas' land. The tract was called Golden Quarter.[22]

Records show that Argoll Yardley, who was the son of the governor of Virginia, imported two slaves, Andolo and Maria, probably from the Spanish Caribbean, when he resided on the Western Shore. At the time of his death in 1655 his inventory showed that he had " towe Negro men, towe Negro women (their wives) one Negro girle aged 15 yeares, Item One Negro aged about teen yeareas and one Negro child aged about sixe moneths...Servants, towe men their tyme three months... one Negro boye about three yeares old(which witness of his godfather) is to bee free at twenty foure yeares of age and then to have towe cowes given him." In 1637 he brought them to Northampton County. Dennise, one of their two daughters was born in 1641. She was sold at age 12 to John Michaels, who lived in that same area.[23]

The evidence of these interconnections supports the supposition that an indentured servant, James Beckett, fathered Peter most probably with the female slave Dennise. This child then had the slave status of his mother, but carried the last name of his father although a slave, and at some point became a part of the household of John Eyre.

Peter Beckett

The first record of Peter Beckett is in 1671 on the Tithable List or tax list in Northampton County, Virginia.[24]. On that list there is no indication of the race of those in the household. Peter's appearance on the list in 1671 would mean therefore, that he was probably sixteen at that time and hence, born in about 1655.

The tithable lists for 1671-1673 no longer exist. The next available tithable list is for 1674, and it shows the first indication that those in the Eyre household, including Peter Beckett, are African-American. This list shows the household as including three Negroes, with no names given. The 1675 Tithable List includes Peter, along with Thomas and Frances Rodriggus (a.k.a. Driggus) in the household of John Eyre. The

1677 Tithable List is the first that specifically describes Peter and Thomas Driggus as Negro.[25]

FREE BORN

Sarah Dawson

The records I found in the actual court documents revealed that Mr. Heinegg had made a mistake in his initial research when he concluded that Peter Beckett married an Elizabeth Kettle and had a son named Kettle Tony. As best I could piece together the information, he had associated the wrong names somehow . There was a mulatto child named Tony born to an Elizabeth Kettle, but they had no relationship to Peter Beckett. Instead the records I found clearly showed Sara Dawson (aka Dason) was the servant Peter married. I contacted Mr. Heinegg about this error, and he agreed that my research was accurate and that if he did another reprint of the book he would correct it.

In the mid 17th century the port of Bristol England had a monopoly on trade with Virginia. The trade in indentured servants was especially heavy at this time., but there was so much fraud that the Bristol City Council passed an ordinance in 1654 requiring that a register of servants destined for the colonies be kept. The purpose was to discourage the infamous practice of coercing or duping innocent youths into servitude known as "spiriting." These registers were called "Servants to Foreign Plantations" and "Actions and Apprentices." Most of these servants came from the West County, the West Midlands or from Wales.

In September 1675 Sarah Dawson and Elizabeth Lowe were two of the servants recorded in those registers. They left Bristol destined for Virginia indentured to Lawrence Herder, a mariner. Sarah's term of indenture was four years and Elizabeth's was for seven years.[26]

In November 1677, Sarah was indentured to John Eyre. As was the practice, he took her to the Northampton County court to have her age judged. The court record states that "This day Major John Eyre brought his servant woman named Sarah Dason to the court to have their judgment of her age whom they adjudged to be sixteen years of age.[27] That would make her date of birth approximately 1661.

Thus Sarah Dawson came to the same Eyre plantation where Peter Beckett was a slave.

Peter and Sarah

It was in this environment that Peter and Sarah came together. Indentured servants were not allowed to marry. During those times, the punishment for "Bastard Baringe" did not depend upon the race of the offenders. Public whipping and extension of their indenture time was the lot of the maidservants found guilty of fornication. From 1662 onward, they had to pay the large sum of two thousand pounds of tobacco, or two years of extra service to their masters for each illegitimate child they bore.

The court records show that seven years later in 1684, Sarah Dawson had three children by Peter for which she was ordered to serve another six years and receive 21 lashes on the shoulders. The order states that:

> Whereas Sarah Dawson, servant to Major John Eyre... acknowledges in open court that she hath had three bastard malotto children by her said Master's Negro slave, Peter. It is therefore the judgement of the court and accordingly ordered that after... her said master six years... for her said offenses and that for the last of the said three offenses the sheriff take her into his custody and... twenty one lashes on her naked shoulders were laid on ....[28]

Sarah and Peter married after the end of her indenture by 1689. This is known because of the court document in which she is referred to as the "wife of Peter Beckett, slave to John Eyre."

The documents states that:

> Upon petition of Sarah the wife of Peter Beckett, slave to major John Eyre it is the judgement of the court and accordingly ordered that her child is at her own disposal there finding sufficient...to hold the parish harmless from the said children as..said shall satisfy the said Eyre for ....expanded and trouble of his house about the said child from its birth to the time of her placing it out[29]

FREE BORN

Although there were many instances of free African-American men marrying white women in this time period on Virginia's Eastern Shore, **Peter is the only slave ever recorded as having married a white woman.**

By 1702 Peter is also free as established in a court document showing that Peter and Sarah, his wife, sued a John Morine. If he were still a slave he would not have had that right to go to court and sue.

Other Free Blacks

Beyond the one court document indicating his freedom, there is not, unfortunately, much more on the records about Peter Beckett. However, there is much more material on several of his contemporaries. Emanuell Driggus, Anthony Johnson, Francis Payne, William Harman, Philip Mongom, Sebastian Cane, and Anthony Longo are examples of free Negroes who did particularly well for themselves and whose lives I know more about from existing documentation. The information that follows presents what I discovered about the lives of these free men and women and will shed light on what life must have also been like for Peter and Sarah Beckett during those times. Much of the information comes from the book by Deal.

The family of Emanuell Driggus is particularly relevant as his descendants and those of Peter and Sarah have intertwined lives in several subsequent generations

Emanuell Rodriggus (a.k.a. Driggus-Driggers)

Emanuell Driggus was the progenitor of a family whose history can be traced over the span of nearly two centuries. Their story is well documented through court records and reveals much about changing race relations and the shifting fortunes of Negro slaves, servants, and freedmen in colonial Virginia.

There are no records on Emanuell Driggus before his arrival in Virginia. He must have arrived in the late 1630s or early 1640s, for in 1645 his master Captain Francis Pott settled in Northampton County, having lived across the bay for 20 years. He took along Negro slaves including Driggus and his wife Frances Bashawe Farnando.

Upon arriving in 1645, Pott had given some cattle to his slave Driggus (cow and a calf) and Farnando(a calf). Owning personal property from which income could be generated was a matter of great importance to these slaves and a cause for controversy in later years. At the same time, Pott agreed to take on-- as servants Driggus --two daughters, Elizabeth (age 8) and Jane (age 1). These may not have been his actual children-documents never show Frances as the mother. Emanuell Driggus had at least three children with Frances: Thomas, Frances and Ann.

In May 1652 he purchased freedom of Jane from Frances Pott. In the fall of the same year, Driggus pressed his master to declare in writing that he and Farnando had cattle, and hogs which they had lawfully gotten and purchased and that they could dispose of them as they pleased.

In 1656 while still a slave, he had given a heifer to a Negro child on the neighboring plantation of Mrs. Anne

Littleton. For a man who was trying to accumulate enough savings to purchase freedom for himself and other members of his own family, this was a generous gesture. Circumstances suggest that the child may have been Driggus' godson.

In 1658 John Pott died. His widow, Susannah, married William Kendall the next year, and with her two sons (including John Eyre by her first husband, Thomas Eyre,) and their slaves, moved from Magothy Bay to the Kendall plantation on Cherrystone Creek. All of the slaves except one-Farnando were freed by Kendall, who declared in court in May 1659 that he was carrying out a verbal request that had inadvertently been omitted from Pott will. There was no mention at all of Farnando's companion and fellow slave, Emanuell Driggus a little more than two years later, a free man, apparently at the behest of Kendall, his new master.

Though the relations with his former master (Pott) had soured, Driggus was apparently able to reach some new understanding with the younger and wealthier Kendall. It was a time of significant changes in Driggus's life. Although he could not sever all connections to his slave past, he became in some respects a very different man.

By October 1661 the Driggus was free and had taken a second wife, Elizabeth. Apparently she was white. The evidence that she was white is circumstantial but strong. Like

Amy Payne, she never appeared on a tithable list with her husband, and at least one of the children, born after Frances Driggus died, was described later in the court records as a mulatto.

The first evidence that he did in fact become a free man is contained in a deed of jointure, dated 1 October 1661, in which Emanuell Driggus "of Accomack planter" gave a three-year-old gray mare and its increase to his wife Elizabeth.

The former owner of Emanuell Driggus, William Kendall, now became his landlord, and in 1665 wrote a lease with a special proviso: The lessees were to be Emanuell Driggus and his wife Elizabeth, and then "the Heiress lawfully begotten of the said Elizabeth, and for want of them... any of the Heiress formerly begotten by the said Rodriggus."

Driggus and his family spent about 10 years on a this 145-acre tract of land. From 1661 until 1664, Emanuell Driggus headed a household that probably included his wife Elizabeth, daughter Jane (aged 17 in 1661), and one other adult of undetermined identity, as well as at least one of the new couple's mulatto children.

FREE BORN

The Becketts and the Drigguses

From the beginning the Becketts and the Driggers (Driggus,Drighouse) families lives were intertwined. Emmanuel Driggus, as explained above, was manumitted by William Kendall who was John Eyre's stepfather. The Negroes on the Tithable List of John Eyre in 1671 included Peter Beckett and Thomas Driggus, Emanuel's son by his first wife. He continued to reside there as a slave with Peter.

Thomas Driggus apparently was not easy to get along with. In 1668 while still in the household of William Kendall he was taken to court for neglecting his masters service.[30] The plaintees included not only his owner but a group of free blacks as well as whites all of whom complained that Driggus had grossly abused them. By 1668 he had married a free black woman, Sara King. They lived together on Kendall's plantation and then on John Eyre's with Peter Beckett.

Peter must have been witness to some interesting behavior. By 1672 there was trouble because Sarah, was not acting like the wife of a slave. Apparently John Eyre took her to court where he got an order that she "shall not depart the house of Mr. John Eyres master of the said Thomas Rodrigus without the leave and order both of her said husband and Mr. John Eyre."[31] Eyre's displeasure at having this independent woman in his household is evident and it seems from the wording of the court order that her husband was also displeased with her behavior.

Two years later Sarah was living on her own, but she continued to keep her husband's name the rest of her life and bore him four or five more children.

Ann Beckett, born 10 December 1697, was the four-year-old daughter of Sarah Becket. She was bound apprentice until the age of 18 years to Mrs. Ann Eyre on 28 July 1702 with her mother's consent.[32] On 20 June 1716 Ann received 25 lashes for having a bastard child by John Drighouse (Driggus) [33]

Her sister, Elizabeth Beckett born about1705, apparently married the same John Drighouse before 1724. She was called Betty Drighouse, tithable in his household from 1724 to 1726, but then was called Betty Beckett again by 1727.

Jean Beckett, born perhaps 1700, was a free negro woman' in the household of Thomas Driggers in the 1727 list of Matthew Harmonson. She was his common-law wife, called Jane Drighouse when she was taxable in his household in 1737 and in 1744 with her daughter, Esther Drighouse. Thomas Drighouse called himself free Negro' in his 21 April 1757 Northampton County will which was proved 14 June 1757.[34] He made Jane (a.k.a. Jean) Beckett his executor and left all he had to her and her three daughters, Hester, Betty, and Lydia Beckett.

Mark Beckett, the bastard child of Ann Beckett and John

Drighouse, married Margaret Drighouse, widow of Azaricum Drighouse.[35] In 1744 he and his wife, Pegg Beckett, were taxable with her son Jacob and he and Peggy were taxables in 1765 and in John Bowdoin's list for 1769.

Anthony Johnson

Of all the free Negroes in the seventeenth-century Virginia, Anthony Johnson has received the most attention. In his lifetime he managed to achieve that goal so illusive to immigrants of all races, the American dream.

By the time Johnson died he had become a freeman, formed a large and secure family, built up a sizable estate, and established himself as the "Negro patriarch" of Pungoteague Creek, a small inlet on the western side of Northampton County.

During the 1640s the Johnsons acquired a modest estate (250 acres). Raising livestock provided a reliable source of income, for at mid-century, especially on the Eastern Shore, breeding cattle and hogs was as important to the local economy as growing tobacco. He probably began to build up his herds during the 1640s. Two hundred and fifty acres was a considerable piece of land by Eastern Shore standards, and though the great planters controlled far more acreage, many people owned smaller tracts or no land at all. Johnson's 250 acres were located on Pungoteague creek.

In February 1653 Johnson's luck appeared to run out. A fire destroyed much of his plantation. This event--the Northampton Court called it "an unfortunate fire"--set off in turn a complicated series of legal actions that sorely tested Anthony's standing within the Pungoteague community, and at one point even jeopardized much of his remaining property. The blaze itself had been devastating.

After the county justices viewed the damage, they concluded that without some assistance the Johnsons would have difficulty in the "obtayneing of their livelyhood," and when Anthony and Mary formally petitioned for relief, the court excused Mary and the Johnsons' two daughters from paying "Taxes and Charges in Northampton County for public use" for "their natural lives." The court's decision represented an extraordinary concession.

The reduction of annual taxes obviously helped Johnson to reestablish himself, and the fact that he was a "Negro" and so described during the proceedings seems to have played no discernible part in the deliberations of local justices. Moreover, the court did more than simply lighten the Johnson's' taxes. By specifically excusing the three Negro women from public levies, the justices made it clear that, for tax purposes at least, Mary and her daughters were the equals of any white women in Northampton County.

FREE BORN

By the mid to late 1660s many of the members of the Johnson family left Virginia and migrated to Somerset County Maryland where they acquired land and named it Angola, suggested by some historians to be homage to remembrance of their ancestors homeland. From there descendants migrated to the Delaware and mixed with marginal Indian and white populations to form a triracial community.

Philip Mongum

Philip Mongum managed to become a relatively prosperous tenant farmer. He may have cultivated a leasehold as early as the mid-1660s, but the records on this point are ambiguous. In any case, in 1678, Mongum and two white men, Edward Parkinson and Peter Duparks, leased a 300-acre plantation from Mary Savage. This land was located on Mattawaman Creek about a third of the way up the Virginia Eastern Shore in Northampton County. It is not certain whether the three men divided their plantation into equal shares. Whatever the nature of their partnership may have been. Mongum quickly doubled his holdings. In 1680 he acquired a 200-acre leasehold on a small creek near the Virginia -Maryland boundary.

Philip Mongum calculated his financial success in terms of livestock. Each horse represented a considerable investment, and when a "light bay mare" disappeared in July 1678, Mongum searched frantically for the lost animal. He later appeared before the Northampton court to post a reward for anyone bringing it back. It is impossible to determine whether this device worked, for the court records never again mention Mongum's prize "light bay."

Most Negroes displayed similar eagerness to obtain cattle. In fact, livestock transactions of this type brought Negro planters before the county justices more often than did any other form of business. Anthony Johnson was an especially active buyer. This extensive cattle trade brought free Negroes into large contact with a large number of white planters whom they normally could not have expected to meet. In other words, these animals provided more than a highly profitable investment, more than a means to ensure financial independence. They became the basis of a complex transactional network involving many persons scattered widely over the Eastern Shore.

Francis Payne

Francis Payne was born perhaps 1620, was a slave called "Francisco a Negroe" when Philip Taylor claimed him as a headright in 1637. The relationship between some masters and their slaves before slavery became institutionalized is illustrated by an agreement between Taylor and one of his slaves who stated in Northampton County Court that:

> Now Mr. Taylor and I have divided our corne and I am very glad of it now I know myne...owne ground I will worke when I please and play when I please.[36]

The life of Francis Payne as a slave and a freedman in Northampton County illustrates how far an individual Negro could go in winning the favor and confidence of some whites in seventeenth-century Virginia . A slave for at least twelve years, Francis Payne began in 1649 to purchase his freedom, which he finally achieved in 1656. He lived as a free man for another seventeen years until his death in 1673.

Thomas Yeoman, a poor white Northampton County planter, called him "Frank Capt. Taylor's Negroe" in 1646 when he bequeathed him his estate consisting of 400 pounds Of tobacco, 3 barrels of corn, and a shirt in gratitude for Francis looking after him while he was sick.[37]

Taylor died the same year and left Francis to his widow Jane who remarried and moved to Maryland with her husband, William Eltonhead . On May 1649 Jane called him "Francis Payne my Negroe servant" when she gave him the right to a crop he was raising and the "power from tyme to tyme to make use of the ground and plantation" in return for 1,500 pounds of tobacco and 6 barrels of corn after the harvest.[38] This land was in Northampton County on Old Town Neck.

A series of notes and declarations by Jane Eltonhead in 1656 finally cleared away all uncertainties about the legal status of Francis Payne as a free Negro. Mrs. Eltonhead, who that year became a widow again when her second husband died, declared for the Northampton County court in July that all differences between Payne and her own family had been settled. Once free, he too married a white woman. They were married in the summer of 1656, for in September of that year,he gave to his "well beloved wife, Amy Payne, "as a jointure, a mare he had bought the year before from a Dutch merchant on the shore.

His wife lived with him until his death seventeen years later. In the spring of 1673, his health failing, Payne drew up his last will and testament. The document provided considerable insight into Payne determination not to lose the few tangible fruits of his hard-won freedom. Childless, he bequeathed his entire estate to his wife Amy, except for some cow calves left to their godchildren.

FREE BORN

LIFE AND TIMES

My research showed that the slaves and free Negroes who lived in Northampton County lived on plantations clustered in a fairly small area near Cherrystone Creek and Magothy Bay in the bottom third of the county. A large proportion of the county's free Negroes congregated in the same areas, rented land from the same planter families, and maintained kin ties and friendships with the slaves, as well as with lower-class white neighbors. Racial segregation was as not much in evidence as was class segregation. As the court records showed, men and women of both races of the servant class drank, smoked, caroused, fought, and slept together.

The court records showed also that, despite hardships, the blacks during this period were a industrious group. They managed to acquire, while slaves, the property and skills that would pave the way for their transition to freedom. With their masters' permission, they kept livestock and worked on their own plots of land, producing surpluses with which they could purchase their freedom. They assimilated the language, customs, and beliefs of the English. They had diverse economic relations with their white and black neighbors. Whether as tenant farmers, carpenters, or hired laborers, most participated in the local economy much as landless white freedmen did.

FREE BORN

Laws and Restrictions

By 1680, the tidewater planters were worried enough about the meetings held by their black bondsmen at plantation gatherings and at burials to usher passage of a law forbidding arms such as clubs, staffs, guns, swords or other weapons to *Negroes* and slaves; furthermore, slaves were forbidden to leave their owner's plantation without a certificate and then only when necessary.

In 1681, the legislature became alarmed at the "inconvenience" to the colony that occurred upon the emancipation of Negroes and mulattos (and its resultant increase in a free Negro population). They feared that these freed slaves might entice other Negroes from their master's service, or become recipients of stolen goods, or be so elderly that the county would have to maintain them. So the legislature passed a law forbidding emancipation of any Negro or mulatto unless the owner paid for his transportation outside Virginia within six months of setting the slave free. This law had the effect of making black bondsmen slaves for life.

In the same year, the legislature passed the first of many laws outlawing intermarriage between an English or other white man or woman, bond or free, to a Negro, mulatto, or Indian man or woman, bond or flee. The penalty was banishment from Virginia. Obviously as evidenced by Peter and Sarah's marriage along with several others, this law like many laws was ignored on the Eastern Shore at least for a short period of time.

In 1696, the colonial legislature reiterated that the condition of children born in Virginia, whether bond or free, was according to the condition of the mother. IF the mother was a free woman of color, the child was free. If the mother was a slave, the child was also a slave.

It probably did not occur to Peter and Sarah that they were living in what would become a racist society. During the period of their lifetime, I found several recorded instances of intermarriage between free blacks and indentured servants so their union was not unique. However both Emmanuel Driggus and Francis Payne before him made over deeds of jointure to their white wives. This suggests that the women wanted to protect themselves against destitution by securing claims to portions, however modest, of the estates of their husbands, who were, after all, newly freed slaves. Although the romantic ingredient in these matches was strong enough for the wives to cross racial lines, it seems they still felt they needed some economic insurance.

Many slaves continued to be manumitted, to purchase their freedom and begin lives as farmers and tradesmen. They recorded wills, accumulated property, and educated their offspring because they believed their families would continue to play the same role in society and have the same possibilities they had. It likely did not occur to them that their white neighbors were gradually making decisions that would reduce them and their future offspring permanently to the lowest levels of society

I found that it was not until after the early 1700's that the status of free blacks had totally deteriorated. What caused this change, why did it happen? Probably the biggest single factor was the growth of the Negro population. Until that time, the total number of Negroes free and slave in all of Virginia remained relatively small.

However, as the supply of white indentured servants diminished, and the increased production of tobacco required more labor, slave traders brought in thousands of new slaves each year. These new slaves originated directly from Africa, not Barbados or the Spanish Caribbean, and they landed in the New World utterly unfamiliar with their master's language or culture.

This massive influx of alien laborers brought about a fundamental change in the character of race relations. The white landowners felt threatened by such a large number of blacks unless they could be totally controlled. If they could become free, this could not continue. Forcing whites to close ranks and crushing the hopes of enslaved blacks went hand in hand.

FREE BORN

A plantation society based upon the exploitation of black slaves was emerging and along with it came increasingly racist attitudes and practices among whites that denied to free blacks the social "space" that they had enjoyed in earlier decades. They could no longer mingle easily with whites and were lumped with slaves and Indians as objects of the ever more repressive legislation of Virginia. Socially and economically marginal, many free blacks tottered on the brink of virtual enslavement. Step by step various liberties that had been permitted to the free black community were abridged or eliminated and their freedom to interact with white neighbors curtailed.

- *In 1705,* alarmed by the numbers of free Negroes who owned slaves, the legislature decreed that no Negro, mulatto, or Indian could purchase any Christian servant, except of their own complexion, as slaves. Negroes were forbidden to purchase any white Christian servant. During the same year, they reaffirmed the restrictions 'in travel, forbidding slaves to leave the plantation on which they lived without a certificate of leave. Slaves were also forbidden weapons. The penalty for disobeying this law was twenty lashes for either offense.
- In 1705, indentured women servants who had illegitimate children by a Negro or mulatto were

liable for a fine for the use of the parish or sale of the servant for five years after the expiration of her original indenture. The children of such a union were to be bound out as servants until they reached the age of thirty-one. Sixty years later, in 1765, the legislature passed a law decreeing that illegitimate children of women servants and Negroes or free Christian white women by Negroes, were to be bound out. The boys were to serve until they reached the age of twenty-one, the girls until they were eighteen.

- In 1723, the legislature addressed emancipation once more. Negroe and Indian slaves could not be set free except for meritorious service was to be so adjudged by the Governor and Council. If slaves were freed without the approval of the Governor and Council, the parish Churchwardens were to sell the emancipated slave at public auction proceeds were then to be applied for the use of the parish. This law remained in effect until after the American Revolution.
- By 1723 the burdens of color had grown great. Though free blacks could not serve with arms in the militia, could not testify under oath against white Christians, could not vote in elections, could not employ white indentured servants, and were deemed

criminals if they struck any white person, even in self defense.

- In 1732 the colonial legislature moved to abolish voting rights for free Negroes and Indians, thus totally denying their voice in determining the laws that determined their fate.
- Also 1732, a group of white planters from the Eastern Shore complained to the Virginia Assembly that the free Negroes had grown too populous. They didn't need them for labor and didn't want them having the opportunities to advance in society. They believed they were dangerous and would influence and assist the slaves to rebellion.
- In 1758 citizens from Northampton County even urged colonial authorities to expel all free Negroes from Virginia. Later a law was passed stating that any manumitted slaves had to leave the state within two years or loose their freedom, but again this law was often ignored on the Eastern Shore.

Changing economic conditions then closed off the few opportunities available to free blacks. As the use of slave labor increased, slaves began to take over the basic artisan functions that had previously been done by free black craftsmen. Without land of their own, most free black men and women had little recourse after 1750 except to work as tenant farmers and hired laborers. This appears to have been the fate of my ancestors.

Unique Life Stories

Although it appears that the majority of subsequent generations of Becketts remained on the Eastern Shore as subsistence farmers, there were two members of the family who managed to escape that routine during the Revolutionary War by becoming sailors.

The first was William Beckett who was born in about 1742 and probably the son of Elizabeth Beckett who had married John Drighouse. In a court record from the period 1775-1803 his brother Peter admitted that he was indebted to the British merchants Atchinson, Hays and Company. In that case he stated that his brother William Beckett had sailed to the West Indies just before the Revolutionary War and had been impressed aboard a British armed ship. He stated that his brother had lived in Dublin, Ireland since that time.[39] One day I would love to research to see if I could discover his fate.

The second Beckett sailor was George Beckett born in about 1760. He was a seaman who served in the Virginia Navy during the Revolutionary War. He died intestate leaving no children. His estate was divided among his four sisters, Nancy, Betty, Rebecca, and Mason and their children.[40]

FREE BORN

"Bounding Out"

I found that choices for marriage, family and work all narrowed considerably. Many free blacks were forced by circumstances or law to spend much of their lives, as children and adults, in the households of white masters and employers. Children whose families could not prove they could support them were routinely taken from their mothers and given over or "bound out" or indentured to someone willing to care for and train them until they became adults. If a mother could not pay the fine for having had a child out of wedlock, she, too, could be bound out as a servant for several years.

In 1765, the colonial legislature passed legislation dealing with apprentice-ships. The House of Burgesses provided apprenticeships for bastard children of women servants and Negroes or free white women by Negroes. Boys were to be "bound out" until they were twenty-one; girls until they were eighteen. The former law apprenticing children until they were thirty-one was thought to be too severe on the children and repealed.

In 1785, legislation provided for district overseers of the poor in each county. The Assembly transferred powers held by the old churchwarden system to the overseers of the poor.

Then, in 1792, the General Assembly passed a law providing for the poor, lame, blind and others who are unable to maintain themselves. They empowered overseers of the poor to provide poor houses, nurses and doctors for the care of the poor.

The county courts directed the overseers of the poor to apprentice poor orphans and children to a person that the court approved. Boys were bound out until they were twenty-one, girls until they were eighteen.

It is partially through the existence of these court records of the "bounding out" of Beckett children from the early 1700s that I was able to trace several subsequent generations of Becketts.. The records revealed how prevalent this practice of "bounding out" was in its impact on the Beckett family. There were records going through three generations into the 1760s as follows:

- Ann Beckett (daughter of Sarah) – age 4-was bound apprentice in July 1702 to Mrs. Ann Eyre until the age of 18.[41]
- Peter Beckett (son of Elizabeth) – age 3- was bound apprentice in Northampton County in 1737/8.[42]
- William Beckett (son of Elizabeth)- age 7 – was bound apprentice on 6 August 1749.[43]
- Isaac Beckett (son of Betty/Elizabeth) – age 13 – was bound apprentice on 25 November 1759.

- William Beckett (son of Rebecca) – age 2- was bound apprentice on 12 December 1723.[44]
- Isaiah Beckett (son of Mark Beckett) – age 12-was bound apprentice in March 1785.[45]
- Leah Beckett (daughter of Sarah born 1721) – age 9- was bound apprentice on 31 August 1748.[46]
- Rachel Beckett (daughter of Sarah born 1721) – age 3 – was bound apprentice to Posthumus Core on May 1746.[47]
- Spencer Beckett (son of Sarah born 1721) – age one – was bound apprentice to William Bradford on 13 Novemebr 1749.[48]
- Betty Beckett (no parent given) – age 16 – was bound apprentice March 1766.[49]
- Comfort Beckett (no parent given) – age 4 – was bound apprentice in December 1757.[50]
- Peter Beckett (no parent given) – age 14 – was bound apprentice in August 1766.[51]
- John Beckett (son of Sarah) – age 3 – was bound apprentice in 1759 to Zerobell Downing.[52]

There are probably many more citations of this practice for the Beckett family for subsequent years, but I have no yet researched them.

FREE BORN

The "Black Codes"

The last two decades of the eighteenth century saw the Virginia General Assembly pass a host of laws relating to free Negroes and to slaves. Following the aftermath of the American Revolution and its ideals engendered by the Declaration of Independence, the Virginia legislature decided to allow emancipation of slaves by deed, will, or other instrument of writing. The document had to be signed, sealed and witnessed.

The former owner was to be responsible for the support of any emancipated slaves not of sound mind and body or over the age of forty-five. Likewise, the emancipator was to be responsible for children- boys under 21 years of age and girls under 18 years of age. A copy of the emancipation was to be given to the freed slave. The penalty for being without a copy was jail, especially if the freed, slave traveled outside the county. Liberated slaves, who could not pay parish or county levies, could be hired out by the Sheriff for as long as it took to raise the taxes they owed.

During this same period, the General Assembly granted immediate emancipation to any Negro slave who had served in the Revolutionary war. For owners neglecting to emancipate these veterans, the General Assembly gave them the right to petition he local County Court for the right to sue for their freedom.

Yet at the same time that the Assembly was loosening some of the bonds on slavery, they were tightening many others. Year by year, law by law, the rights of the free blacks diminished. Collectively these restrictive laws cam to be known as the "Black Codes." A partial list is described as follows.[53]

- In 1785, the General Assembly enacted legislation prescribing slaves from traveling from his residence, without a license or a letter showing he has permission to do so from his master. Slaves were also forbidden to keep arms; riots and unlawful assemblies were punishable by whipping.
- In 1792 Negroes and mulattos were forbidden to carry firearms although free Negroes could be permitted gun; Negroes, bond or free, living on the frontier could be licensed to carry a gun.
- In 1792, there were a variety of other laws passed: conspiracy to rebel or make or cause an insurrection, became a felony punishable by death. Negro and mulatto slaves were adjudged to be personal estate. Slaves were not to trade as free men. Intermarriage between a Negro man or woman and a free white man

or woman was punishable by a six month jail term. The legislature levied a $30.00 fine on the parties involved an, $250.00 fine on the minister.

- In 1793 proved to be as busy. The legislature voted to stop the practice of Negro slaves from hiring out as free persons and to keep a closer eye on the free Negro populations found through out the local communities in the Commonwealth. Slave holders had tended to allow their Negro slaves to hire themselves out, especially those who were skilled artisans. Now, the legislature forbade this practice; owners of these "quasi-free" slaves could be indicted by a grand jury for hiring their slaves out contrary to law; the Negro slave found himself in jail while the owner was hauled into court and made to pay jail fees.
- In 1806, free Negroes were prescribed from carrying a "firelock" of any kind without a license.
- In 1795 the General Assembly passed legislation to register all free Negroes and mulattos in the Commonwealth with the clerk of the Court in the community in which they lived, who were free to sell their services, were to be registered and numbered in a book kept by the town Clerk This register recorded

name, age, color, status and emancipation details-by whom and in which county court the registrant had been freed.

- In 1801, the state legislature decreed that county commissioners of revenue were to return a complete list of all free Negroes in their districts on an annual basis. This list was to contain names, gender, residence and trade of each free Negro. A copy of the list was to be posted on the door of the county court house. If a registered free Negro moved to another county, then magistrates there could issue a warrant for him, unless he was employed. Otherwise, he would be jailed as a vagrant.
- In 1806, the General Assembly moved to remove the free Negro population from Virginia with a law that stated that all emancipated slaves, freed after May 1, 1806, who remained in the Commonwealth for more than a year, would forfeit his right to freedom and be sold by the Overseers of the Poor for the benefit of the parish. Families wishing to stay were to petition the legislature through the local county court.
- In 1823, any flee Negro who was convicted of an offense punishable by imprisonment for more than two years, was now punished by whipping and sold as

a slave and banished from Virginia, at the discretion of the Court or a jury. If free Negroes or slaves willfully assaulted and beat a white person with intent to kill and was convicted of this offense, they too could be punished by a public whipping and banishment from the state. If the convicted person returned to Virginia, he or she could be hung.

- After the failure of the Nat Turner slave rebellion in 1830, the Virginia General Assembly passed a variety of laws curtailing slave and free Negroes' right to assembly. To prevent free Negroes from assembling ant speaking at church, the legislature forbade preaching by slaves, free Negroes or mulattos at religious meetings. Indeed free people of color and slaves were forbidden to hold any religious meeting during the day or evening. The penalty for violating this ordinance was a public whipping of thirty-nine lashes.
- Slaves attending religious meetings without the consent of their master were also liable to a public whipping. However, religious instruction to slaves of free Negroes could be given during the day by a licensed white minister and the slaves of any one owner could assemble for religious instruction during the day.

FREE BORN

- In 1832, the Assembly addressed riots, unlawful assembly, trespass, sedition, and conspiracy to commit insurrection. If slaves or free *Negroes* wrote or printed anything advising people of color to commit insurrection or rebellion, the perpetrators were to be whipped. The same penalty was instituted for riots, unlawful assembly, trespass and seditious speeches.
- During the same year, the legislature prohibited Negroes from selling or giving away liquor near any public assembly. The penalty for violating this law was also a public whipping.
- Another law passed in 1832 curtailed the rights of free people of color to own slaves. After this date, no free Negro would be able to acquire ownership of any slave, except through inheritance, other than his or her spouse or children.
- In 1843, the legislature curtailed slave and free Negro rights to dispense medicine. Selling, preparing or administering medicine became a misdemeanor whose penalty was a public whipping. Preparations of drugs by free Negroes that caused abortions carried a penalty of five to ten years in prison. If slave prepared a drug to cause abortion, the first time offender

received a public whipping. Any offense after that was a hanging offense.

- In 1846, the General Assembly granted justices of the peace the right to try any free Negro who committed simple larceny or offenses valued $20.00. If convicted, the free Negro faced a public whipping of thirty-n lashes. If acquitted, the acquittal was final. If a free person of color assaulted a white person with intent to kill, conviction carried with it a prison term between five and eighteen years
- In 1858 free people of color could not buy wine or ardent spirits unless they had written permission from three or more justices that they were sober, orderly and of good character. In 1860, free Negroes could not be ordinary or tavern keepers and were prescribed from selling hard liquor.
- In 1858 Free Negroes could now own slaves only through inheritance.
- In 1860, the legislature decreed that flee Negroes who committed offenses punishable by imprisonment in the penitentiary could be, at discretion of the county court, sold into absolute slavery.

Just viewing all those laws one after the other and imagining their impact on the day to day lives of my ancestors is overwhelming. It never ceases to amaze me that they managed to endure and avoid re enslavement, imprisonment or worse.

FREE BORN

THE BECKETTS AFTER PETER AND SARAH

Because Sarah was free, her children were born free, as were their descendants through the female line. Although the free black women could marry, the number of potential free husbands was quite small and the difficulties of arranging and maintaining formal marriages with slave men were immense. Some of the Beckett women may have married slaves, some may have born children outside of formal marriage. However, these hard facts did make tracing subsequent generations before emancipation easier because the family name remained Beckett through the female generations. If the males married or had children with a slave woman, the children would have been slaves and there would not have been records to follow.

The records indicate that by the eighteenth century some of the Becketts had followed the example of the Johnsons and moved up the Delmarva Peninsula to mix with the established triracial communities there. I have not yet researched these lines thoroughly, as I knew I was descended from those that stayed in Virginia until the 1890s.

I found no records of the three children born to Sarah by 1684 for which she had received the twenty-one lashes. They could have died before adulthood, which would not have been uncommon. The four daughters, Ann, Jean, Betty and Rebecca on whom records do exist were born from about 1697 to 1705- up to twenty years after the first three. It is even possible, given those dates, that these were instead the children a daughter named Sarah, but as I found no evidence of this, I have assumed that these four were born later in their lives.

To establish my entire family line I used several types of sources. These included the court records of the "bounding outs" through the 1760s, the Tithable Records, the 1832 list of free blacks, the inheritance of the sailor George Beckett, and the census records. As the census records did not list the children's names until 1850, I had to make some suppositions for generations five and six. To do this I evaluated the approximate ages and the naming conventions. The list that follows represents the line of descendants from the very first blacks on the Eastern Shore of Virginia through thirteen generations down to me.

My grandmother Recie Beckett left Accomack in the late 1890s and went first to Philadelphia, Pennsylvania and then to Riderwood, Maryland. Her sisters, Annie and Lottie, also left and migrated to Philadelphia. But many relatives did stay. To this day there remain Becketts in Accomack and Northampton Counties, three hundred and fifty years after James Beckett and the first Africans arrived on the Eastern Shore of Virginia.

FREE BORN

BECKETT ANCESTORS

First Generation - Andolo And Maria

Second Generation - James Beckett And Dennisse

Third Generation - Peter Beckett

Peter and Sarah had four children of which I found records. These children were:

- Ann Beckett - born 10 December 1697.
- Jean /Jane Beckett- born perhaps 1700.
- Betty Beckett - born around 1705.
- Rebecca/Beck Beckett- born perhaps 1708.

Fourth Generation

Ann Beckett

Ann was born 10 December 1697. She was the 4-year-old daughter of Sarah Beckett who was bound apprentice until the age of 18 years to Mrs. Ann Eyre on 28 July 1702 with her mother's consent.[54] On 20 June 1716, Ann received 25 lashes for having a bastard child by John Drighouse.[55] Her children were:

- William Beckett, born about 1714, a 10-16 year old boy in John Robbins' Northampton County Household from 1724 to 1730.
- Nancy,Beckett born say 1715, taxable in Esther Map's household in 1731.
- Mark,Beckett born say 1716, perhaps Ann's child by John Drighouse. He was a boy not yet tithable in Mark Freshwater's household in the 1725 list of John Robins and taxable in Ann Dod's household in Robins' 1737 list. He married Margaret Drighouse, widow of Azaricum Drighouse.[56] Their son was Isaac born about 1773 and bound apprentice March 1785.[57]

Jean/Jane Beckett

Jean Beckett was born in about 1700. She was a free negro woman tithable in the household of Thomas Driggers (aka Drighouse) in 1727. She was his common-law wife, called Jane Drighouse, when she was taxable in his household in 1737, and with her daughter Ester Drighouse in 1744. Thomas Drighouse made her the executor of his will in 1757 and left all he had to her and her three daughters.[58] Her children were:

- Sarah Beckett, born perhaps 1720, taxable in Thomas Drighouse's household from 1737 to 1741, perhaps deceased by 1757 when her father made his will.
- Comfort Beckett, born perhaps 1723, tithable in Thomas Drighouse's household in 1739 and 1740. She married Jacob Morris by 1743.
- Ester(Hester)Beckett, born perhaps 1724, a tithable in her parents' house hold in the 1744 list of Thomas Preeson.
- Betty Beckett
- Lydia Beckett

Betty/Elizabeth Beckett

Betty/Elizabeth Beckett was born about 1705. She was married to John Drighouse before 1724. This is the same John Drighouse that her sister, Ann, had a child by in 1716. She was called Betty Drighouse from 1724-1726, but was called Betty Beckett in 1727. In 1728 she had apparently moved out of his house and was tithable in John Robin's household. She showed in tithable records to 1744.

Her children were:

- Peter Beckett born about 1735, 3 years old in February 1737/8 when he was bound apprentice in Northampton County.[59]
- William Beckett, born about 1742, a 7 year old bound apprentice on 6 August 1749.[60]
- Issac Beckett born about 1746.

Rebecca/Beck Beckett

Rebecca Beckett, born perhaps 1708, was taxable in Jonathan Stott's household in 1724 and 1725, tithable in the household of (her brother-in-law) John Drighouse in 1726, and in Joachim Michael's household from 1729 to 1743. There is no record of a marriage. As her children retained her last name, it is possible that their father was a slave or that she never married. Her children were:

- William Beckett, born in 1721 bound apprentice on 12 December 1723.[61]
- Sarah Beckett, born perhaps 1721, was a tithable in Jonathan Bell's household in 1737, tithable with (her brother) Peter Beckett in Peter Dowty's

household in 1740. Sarah petitioned the Northampton County Court on 13 November 1749 to bind her child

- Spencer Beckett to William Bradford of Accomack County.[62] She was also the mother of:
- Leah Beckett, born about 1739, a 9 year old bound apprentice August 1748[63] .
- Rachel Beckett, born about 1743, bound apprentice to Posthumous Core on 25 May 1746.[64]
- Betty Beckett, born about 1750
- Comfort Beckett, born about 1753
- Peter Beckett, born about 1752
- John Beckett born September 1756
- Peter Beckett, born perhaps 1723, tithable in Peter Dowty's household in Joachim Michael's list for 1739.
- Isaac Beckett, born perhaps 1726.
- Solomon Beckett, born perhaps 1727.

Fifth Generation - Solomon Beckett

Solomon Beckett was tithable in Joachim Michael's household in 1744, taxable with (his wife) Peggy Beckett in 1765, and a "mulatto" taxable on a tithe and three cattle in

Northampton County in 1787.[65] Most probably he was the father of

- Solomon Beckett born perhaps 1740.

Sixth Generation - Solomon Beckett

Solomon was a free "Negro" tithable in Accomack County in 1797.[66] He was head of a St. George Parish, Accomack County household of seven "other free" in 1800, living near Jo. Stringer's.[67]

He may have been the father of:

- George Beckett, Born perhaps 1760, a seaman from Accomack County who served in the Revolution and died intestate leaving no children. His estate was divided among his four sisters, Nancy, Betty, Rebecca, and Mason.[68]
- Nancy Beavans, born perhaps 1762, deceased by 24 February 1834 when George's estate was divided among her five children. The same court order referred to her as " the said Mary".[69] Her children named in the court order were Solomon Beavans, Thomas Beavans, Peter Beavans, Mary Beavans, and John Beavans.
- Rebecca Beckett, born perhaps 1766, was deceased by 24 February 1834 when George Beckett's estate was divided among her 3 children.
- Betty Beckett, born perhaps 1764.

FREE BORN

Seventh Generation - Betty Beckett

Betty was deceased by 24 February 1834 when her brother George's estate was divided among her four children. As her children retained her last name, again as in prior generations it is possible that either she never married or her husband was a slave and so the children retained her name. Her children were

- Peter Beckett born about 1783
- Rosey Beckett born about 1784
- Nancy Beckett born about 1785
- Rachel Beckett born 1786

Eighth Generation -Rachel Beckett

- Betty's daughter Rachel had a son named Peter Beckett in 1804.[70]

Ninth Generation - Peter Beckett

Peter married Rosey Beavans in 1831. One of their children was

- Major George Beckett who was born in about 1851.[71]

FREE BORN

Tenth Generation -Major Beckett

Major George Beckett was married to Jane. Their children were:

- Recie Inez Beckett born in 1879
- Annie Beckett born in 1884
- Lottie Beckett born in 1886
- Thomas Beckett born in 1890
- Ed Beckett born in 1893

Eleventh Generation - Recie Inez Beckett

Recie left Accomack in the late 1890s and went to Riderwood, Maryland where she met and married William Thomas Adams in early 1900. They had seven children:

- Elton Adams born 1900
- John Adams born 1902
- Annabelle Adams born 1905
- Mabel Adams born 1907
- William Thomas Adams born 1908
- Elizabeth Adams born 1918
- Gertrude Adams born 1919

FREE BORN

Twelfth Generation - William Thomas Adams

William Thomas Adams married Mary Penny Jenkins in 1928.

They had eight children:

- Thomas Adams born in 1929
- Mary Adams born in 1931
- William Crawford Samuel Adams born in 1933
- Sarah Adams born in 1935
- Grace Adams born in 1938
- Allen Adams born in 1940
- Kathleen Adams born in 1943
- Maynard Adams born in 1954

Thirteenth Generation - William Crawford Samuel Adams

FREE BORN

Great Grandfather Major Beckett

Great Grandmother Jane Beckett - Recie's Mother

Grandmother Recie Beckett as Young Girl

Great Grandmother Sara Drake Adams

FREE BORN

Great Uncle Nick and Great Aunt Mary Adams

FREE BORN

Grandfather and Grandmother Adams (c. 1950s)

FREE BORN

THE ADAMS FAMILY

FREE BORN

THE TRIP

After I discovered the Beckett ancestry, I started research on the Adams genealogy. Before starting to search the records though we took another research trip to the Eastern Shore to find McDaniel where Granddad had lived before coming to Riderwood. While driving across the Bay Bridge, I remembered making that same trip on the ferry with my Granddad in the days before the bridge. I had gone to my Uncle Nick's house on Mack's Lane to pick huckleberries. I drove through the towns of Easton and St. Michaels and then found Mack's Lane and Uncle Nick's house.

I remembered that my father's Cousin Helen still lived in the area. So I went back out Mack's Lane to the main road to check at the Post Office. The clerk in the office wasn't able to help me, but she suggested that I check at the Methodist Church just "back up the road a way."

Then I got lucky, because there were several people gathered in the church yard cleaning up after a dinner. Not only did they know Helen, but one man said he would show me where she lived. He got in his car and led me a few miles back toward St. Michaels to her house.

"I know you're an Adams. You must be Bill's son," was Cousin Helen's response as she opened her door to us.

I spent several hours talking with her as she served us a delicious lunch of crab cakes and fresh vegetables. I learned that her mother was Ethel Adams, my great grandfather's sister. Ethel married Robert Caldwell and they had 15 children

When I asked her about her parents, she told me that her father was a waterman in the winter months, planted crops in the summer, raised turkeys and was the first black in Talbot County to drive a school bus.

Links to Frederick Douglass

She showed me a picture of "Hatton Farm" where she grew up and that had been purchased by her parents in the 1920s. Later, Ifound that this "Hatton Farm" figured prominently in the life of Frederick Douglass. After returning from living in Baltimore, it was on this very farm that he was sent by his master to work for Edward Covey. Covey, who farmed this land then, was known as a harsh overseer.

Douglass' biographer tells of how he had walked the seven miles from St. Michaels up the long lane to Covey's house that stood near the shoreline. Although the water has reclaimed much of that shoreline, part of the house is still there today, as is the lane up which he walked.

The research also revealed that while working for Covey, Douglass set up a clandestine school. One of the known students was a Charles (Handy) Caldwell. I believe that he was probably Helen's father's ancestor.

FREE BORN

One More Discovery

Helen was also able to give me another family resource. She said that her cousin, Marie Brooks, would probably remember more family information because her grandfather, James Adams, raised her. James was my great-grandfather's brother. When I visited Marie in Annapolis she was able to give me some valuable information.

She remembered her Grandfather telling her, "My father always told me that he had been born free and had bought each of his children out of slavery when they were born." She also remembered that her Grandfather had said his father's name was George, and that he had been born in Preston in Caroline County.

Now I had the information I needed to go back at least one more generation. The next trip was to the Hall of Records in Annapolis to look for a George Adams in Caroline County.

FREE BORN

DEEPER INTO THE ARCHIVES

There, in the 1850 Census for Caroline County, I found the following:

George Adams - free Negro, age 40
Mary - wife, age 35
Susanna
James
William
George III
Elisah
Mary.

This had to be my Great-Great-Grandfather. Based on the age listed, he would have been born in about 1810. Here was proof that the Adams ancestors were also among those who were free before the Civil War!

I found the next piece of evidence of George's existence in the records of the Caroline County Certificates of Freedom. These Certificates resulted from a Maryland law passed in 1805 that required all free Negroes to register with county officials to prove they were free. The certificate included the individual's name, described his physical appearance, detailed the circumstances of his or her grant of freedom and required a white cosigner who would attest to the information.

FREE BORN

A freedman cherished his "Freedom Paper," keeping it in a safe place such as a watertight tobacco tin. Torn and tattered, he carried it with him at all times because it assured his ability to move about and he might have to prove his free status upon request.

The documents I was looking at were the copies kept in the court records. A huge ledger book contained hundreds of these court copies of the certificates of freedom. They weren't alphabetized or indexed, so I spent several hours deciphering the handwriting page by page. Suddenly my eyes were drawn like a magnet to the name "George Adams and I saw:

> "...a Negro man named George Adams applied for a certificate of freedom under the oath of Charles Edele, free born and raised in Caroline County, black complexion, 5' 10" ... a scar under his right knee caused by the cut of a cycle, marks on nose caused by the small pock."

Here was the freedom certificate of my Great-Great Grandfather complete with a description and evidence that he had been a victim of smallpox!

The Talbot County Certificates of Freedom weren't preserved, but another informative source, the "List of Free Negroes" was. This list contained the names of all free Negro households and their family members in 1832. There was no

George Adams of the correct age listed, although there were several Adams families who were probably relatives. This would have been consistent with the information that George Adams was in Caroline County at that time.

On the far left side of each page of the Talbot County list was a column which was to be checked if the individual indicated a desire to immigrate to Africa. Not surprisingly, none of those listed were interested in this deal.

I continued to look through all the census records for Caroline County. George Adams was listed there in 1830, 1820, and 1810. This would have placed his date of birth sometime before 1775. Also listed were Josh Adams and Rumford Adams. I concluded that one of these men, most probably George, was my Great-Great-Great Grandfather.

There was even a free black Adams in the very first census of 1790 in Talbot County. His name was Samuel Adams and, although I was unable to locate any farther documented proof, I believe that the subsequent free Adams families were related to him.

Next, I went to the Caroline County Library and Courthouse to search marriage and birth records. Here I found a record of the marriage William Adams to Sarah Drake on August 17,1874. Now I knew my great-grandmother's maiden name. An earlier list also showed a marriage registration for a George Adams and Mary Webb on January 17, 1842. I thought it quite likely that this was my Great-Great- Grandfather and Grandmother. Later I learned that this supposition was supported by information that Mr. Webb, in Lutherville, was a relative.

ORIGINS

Now I set out to find if there was any evidence of the origins of the slaves in the Talbot/Caroline county area. My research showed that the majority of the Eastern Shore's slaves came between the years of 1690-1770. During that time the British Royal African Trading Company imported over 100,000 slaves into the Chesapeake region. Almost all of these slaves had been captured in the region of Africa known as the Bight of Biafra in what is now Nigeria. They were from the Ibo, Moko and Efkin tribes.

They were brought over in two waves. The first wave was in the period 1700 to 1739 when the British Royal African Company imported about 60 percent of the total. The second wave came between 1740 and 1770. After that the need declined to the extent that only about 800 slaves a year were imported.

I searched for any evidence to show where the slaves had arrived and who bought them. I found that in Maryland the slave ships were able to go to many of the local Eastern

Shore ports or even directly to many of the plantations instead of a centralized port.

Records showed that the ports of Oxford and Cambridge were the points of entry for most of the slaves who came to the upper Eastern Shore. At that time the town of Oxford was a thriving city and so I concluded it most likely that my ancestors arrived there.

FREEDOM

Even though I now knew the Adams ancestors had been free as far back as the late 1700's, I didn't know where the name came from and how the first Adams had become free. Hoping to find records of manumissions or inventories of slaves, I searched for any Adams in Talbot or Caroline County who was a slave owner. Research showed that only a few large landowners such as the Lloyds or the Tilghmans had any significant numbers of slaves large enough to keep inventories. I found, instead, that most families owned only one or two slaves.

Complicating the search was the fact that Caroline County did not exist before 1774 when it was created from parts of Dorchester and Queen Anne's Counties. The records of Dorchester County prior to that time revealed a Daniel

Adams who had manumitted his two slaves "to satisfy my conscience relative to the keeping of slaves."

I could not find any documentation linking these individuals to my ancestors, nor could I find any other documentation or wills or manumissions that established any links to any of the free Adams families.

Research told me, though, that freed slaves generally chose names that would link the different generations of the families and that less than 20 percent took the names of their masters. At some point, these names may have been taken from a white owner as a way of identifying the location of the family group, but most regarded themselves as having a different name from their masters.

Manumissions

Farther research about free blacks in Maryland revealed that most in that area of the Eastern Shore were manumitted or freed by their owners during the period 1770-1800. There were several laws pertaining to the manumission of slaves in Maryland that are reflected in the data. First, in 1752, a law was passed which provided that persons under land and seal with two witnesses may grant freedom to a slave, if not indebted to creditors and if slave is not over 50 years of age and able to live by work. Then in 1815, a new manumission law was enacted which stated that freedom could be granted to a slave if under 45 years of age, in good health, able to care for self and earn a living.

My research revealed that there were several major reasons for the increase in manumissions in the eighteenth century. The first was economic. By that time the labor-intensive crop of tobacco was no longer economically viable, and the farmers had switched to other crops such as wheat and corn. Then they no longer needed the large numbers of slaves.

The second factor was religion. This time period saw the birth of Methodism on the Eastern Shore. Its original doctrines forbid the ownership of slaves, as did that of the Quakers. Many of the members of these religions manumitted their slaves during this period.

The last factor was the influence of the spirit of the American Revolution. Many patriots truly espoused the concept of liberty for all and freed their slaves.

As the first Adams was free before the 1790 census, I concluded his freedom came during this period. This trend of manumissions continued until by 1860, 53% of all blacks on the Eastern Shore were free. In Caroline County the total was closer to 80%. So the first George Adams would have lived with many other free blacks. I then wondered what was their life like during this time.

Restrictions and Laws[72]

Records show that the white citizens were very concerned and threatened by the presence of so many free blacks which made distinguishing them from slaves and controlling the slaves difficult. Whites especially feared free blacks consorting with slaves, implanting ideas of freedom and helping them to escape. But even as they complained of their presence, unlike in Virginia, the white landowners objected to proposals to make the free negroes leave Maryland, because they needed their labor to harvest the crops.

But just as in Virginia, the Maryland state and local legislatures passed many restrictive laws over the years which collectively were known as the known as "black codes.

Vagrancy, Residency Laws and Freedom Certificates

- In 1796 a statue provided that any free negro who should be found guilty of going at large and living without visible means of support might be complied to give a bond for thirty dollars for his good behavior or leave the state for five days. If he refused to comply he was liable to imprisonment and if he failed to pay to be sold into servitude for six months.

- In 1825 the term allowed for leaving the state increased to fifteen days, or if he refused to comply.
- As vessels travelling the many navigable waters of Maryland afforded an easy means of escape, in 1753 a special regulation was passed forbidding concealment or employment of a slave or servant on board a vessel without his master's consent. Another act in 1824 required ships' masters to keep registers of all colored persons employed on their vessels and prohibited them from carrying out of state any negro or mulatto who did not have a certificate of freedom.
- In the 1830s there was a concern that some vessels were commanded by negro captains and manned by negro crews, thus making it easier to help other slaves escape. A new statue was passed requiring that a white person above the age of eighteen should be the chief navigator on each vessel working in the waters of Maryland.
- In 1796 the legislature enacted a provision that any free negro who should sell or give a certificate of freedom and thereby enable a slave to escape from service, should be liable to a fine of a hundred and fifty dollars, one half of which was to go to the slave's owner.

- In 1805 due to so much fraudulent activity dealing with the freedom certifications, an acted was passed to confine the issuance of freedom certificates to the clerks of the county courts, registers of wills. The papers were to contain a description of the person, age, times of manumission and places of origin.
- In 1807 a statue was passed that made it an offence to be penalized by a fine of ten dollars a week for any non-resident free negro to come into the state and remain longer than two weeks. The intruder could be sold into servitude if he couldn't pay the fine. Exceptions were made for sailors and wagoneers.

Economic Laws

- It was reported that in Worcester County it was reported that free negro participation had become an injury to the oyster industry, so in 1852 negroes engaged in that industry were especially restricted.
- In 1852 a bill applying to Anne Arundel, Somerset and Worcester counties was passed that excluded negroes from holding retailers licenses and several were passed locally excluding them from holding liquor licenses.

FREE BORN

- An act of 1747 forbade the sale of liquor to servants, negroes within three miles of any Quaker meeting in Talbot County.
- In 1831 no retailer was allowed to sell any liquors to any negro anywhere in the state, unless the purchaser bore a permit for the purchase. During the next session, however, it was reported that this law had been a complete failure.
- In 1805 it was reported that free negroes had been selling farm produce which they had received from the hands of slaves. A statue of that year denied to any free negro the right to sell corn, wheat or tobacco without having first procured from the justice of the peace a license stating that the seller was of good character.
- In 1825 the legislature authorized a fine of a hundred dollars on any purchaser of tobacco from a negro unless he had a specialized authorization.
- In the Act of 1831 these restrictive laws were widened to apply to sales of bacon, beef, pork, oats and rye unless the negro seller had a certification proving he had come by the produce honestly.

FREE BORN

Legal rights

- The free negro did have the right to maintain actions at law in the Maryland court with restrictions. With respect to giving evidence in court they were limited. In 1717 a statue was passed restricting admission of negro evidence where a Christian white person was a party. In 1801 slaves were permitted to testify against free negroes charged wither with stealing or receiving stolen evidence.
- The free negroes did enjoy the right to own property. The only exceptions were dogs and guns. In 1715 a law was passed forbidding any negro or other slave to carry a gun away from his master's premises without his permission. In 1806 the legislature prohibited even the keeping of a gun or a dog by a slave and that a free negro at large with a gun had to forfeit it unless he had a magistrate's certificate. The free negro could also procure a license yearly from a justice allowing him to keep only one dog which anybody might kill if kept at large.
- Under the Constitution of 1776 free negroes were allowed to vote at elections for members of the lower house of the legislature. For those freed before 1783

> this privilege continued for another 25 years. But a statute of that date denied to persons manumitted thereafter the privilege of office holding, voting, and giving evidence against white persons and all other rights EXCEPT acquiring and holding property.

The one right that was not denied to them was the right to own land. I now understood why hard work and owning property had been so important to Granddad Adams!

FREE BORN

SUMMARY

I traced the Adams ancestors to a time before the Revolutionary War and in the process discovered much about the life of free blacks and the Eastern Shore of Maryland. Although I couldn't find documented evidence of the origin of any slave ancestors, I did learn enough to draw some general conclusions. And I realized how much more I had to research. There are more sources to check for manumissions such as the Chattel Records of Dorchester and Caroline County. I haven't yet even begun to research any of the genealogy of the female ancestors. What I did discover is summarized in the chart that follow.

FREE BORN

ADAMS ANCESTORS

First Generation

1. George[2] Adams *(SAMUEL[1])* was born 1772 in Caroline County[1], and died Unknown. He married Eliza.

Children of George Adams and Eliza Adams are:

2. i. George[3] Adams, b. 1810, Caroline County.
   ii. Charles Adams, b. 1800.
   iii. William Adams, b. 1809.
   iv. Daniel Adams, b. 1805; m. Mary Harris, 01/01/1830[2].
   v. Noah Adams, b. 1803.

Second Generation

2. George[3] Adams *(GEORGE[2], SAMUEL[1])* was born 1810 in Caroline County[3]. He married Mary Webb 01/17/1842 in Caroline County[4].

Children of George Adams and Mary Webb are:

3. i. William Thomas[4] Adams, b. 01/1848, Preston, Caroline County, MD; d. Unknown.

4. ii. James Adams, b. 1844, Preston, Caroline County, MD; d. 1931.

iii. Elisah Adams, b. 03/13/1859, Mc Daniel, Talbott County, Maryland[5]; d. 02/23/1917, Mc Daniel, Talbott County, Maryland; m. ROSIE.

iv. Mary Adams, b. 1849[6].

v. George Adams, b. 1852, Caroline County[7]; d. 03/30/1904, Talbot County, Witman; m. Henrietta.

vi. Rose Adams, b. Unknown.

Third Generation

3. William Thomas[4] Adams *(GEORGE[3], GEORGE[2], SAMUEL[1])* was born 01/1848 in Preston, Caroline CountyMD, and died Unknown. He married Sarah Drake 08/17/1874 in Talbot County, daughter of Emery Drake and Hannah Turner.

Children of William Adams and Sarah Drake are:

i. Charles Nicholas[5] Adams, b. 1875[8]; m. (1) MARY; M. (2) ELLA.

5. ii. William Thomas Adams, b. 10/18/1877, Mc Daniels, Talbot County, MD; d. 03/17/1963, Lutherville, Baltimore County, MD.

iii. Robert Adams, b. 1878[9].

iv. May Adams, b. 1881[10].

v. Howard Adams, b. 1882[11].

vi. Ernest Adams, b. 1884[12].

vii. Wesley Adams, b. 1886.

viii. Nora Adams, b. 1890[13].

ix. Carroll Adams, b. 1893[14].

x. Grace Adams, b. 1895[15].

6. xi. William Thomas Adams, b. 10/18/1877, Mc Daniels, Talbot County, MD; d. 03/17/1963, Lutherville, Baltimore County, MD.

4. James[4] Adams *(GEORGE[3], GEORGE[2], SAMUEL[1])* was born 1844 in Preston, Caroline County, MD[16], and died 1931[17]. He married Malinda Ward.

Children of James Adams and Malinda Ward are:

i. Ernest Adams[5] , b. Unknown.

ii. Nathan Adams, b. Unknown.

7. iii. Flosie Adams, b. Unknown.

iv. Levi Adams, b. Unknown.

v. Hanson Adams, b. Unknown.

vi. Leslie Adams, b. Unknown.

vii. Irvin Adams, b. Unknown.

viii. Victor Adams, b. Unknown.

ix. Lulu Adams, b. Unknown.

x. Thomas Adams, b. Unknown.

8. xi. Ethel Adams, b. 03/25/1883; d. 05/1943.

Fourth Generation

5. William Thomas[5] Adams *(WILLIAM THOMAS[4], GEORGE[3], GEORGE[2], SAMUEL[1])* was born 10/18/1877 in Mc Daniels, Talbot County, MD[18], and died 03/17/1963 in Lutherville, Baltimore County, MD. He married (1) Mary E. Elles. He married (2) Theresa I. Beckett, daughter of Major Beckett and Jane Beckett.

Children of William Adams and Recie Beckett are:

9. i. Elton[6] Adams, b. 12/08/1900, Lutherville, Balt. Co. MD; d. 11/1993, Lutherville.

10. ii. John Carroll Adams, b. 09/03/1902, Lutherville; d. 07/09/1990, Lutherville.

11. iii. Annabelle Adams, b. 1905; d. 1928.

12. iv. Mabel Adams, b. 1907.

13. v. William Thomas Adams Jr., b. 08/25/1908, Lutherville, MD; d. 02/04/1990, Lutherville, MD.

vi. Elizabeth Adams, b. 1918, 1918.

vii. Gertrude Adams, b. 1919.

7. Flosie[5] *(JAMES[4] ADAMS, GEORGE[3], GEORGE[2], SAMUEL[1])* was born Unknown. She married BROOKS.

Children of Flosie and Brooks are:

i. Marie[6] Brooks, b. 1911.

ii. Flosie E. Brooks, b. 1914.

iii. Eleanor Priscilla Brooks, b. 1922.

iv. John W. Brooks, b. Unknown.

v. Dorothy Mae Brooks, b. Unknown.

vi. Hanson E. Brooks, b. Unknown.

vii. Celestine Brooks, b. Unknown.

viii. Arthur L. Brooks, b. Unknown.

8. Ethel[5] *(JAMES[4] ADAMS, GEORGE[3], GEORGE[2], SAMUEL[1])* was born 03/25/1883, and died 05/1943. She married Robert Caldwell.

Children of Ethel and Robert Caldwell are:

i. Catherine[6] Caldwell, b. Unknown.

ii. James Caldwell, b. Unknown.

iii. Hanson Caldwell, b. Unknown.

iv. Ethel Caldwell, b. Unknown.

v. R. Alphonso Caldwell, b. Unknown.

vi. Stanley Caldwell, b. Unknown.

vii. Helen Caldwell, b. Unknown.

viii. F. Randolph Caldwell, b. Unknown.

ix. Lula Caldwell, b. Unknown.

x. Charles Caldwell, b. Unknown.

xi. Norwood Caldwell, b. Unknown.

xii. Bernard Caldwell, b. Unknown.

xiii. Edith Mae Caldwell, b. Unknown.

xiv. Twins, b. Unknown.

Fifth Generation

9. Elton[6] Adams *(WILLIAM THOMAS[5], WILLIAM THOMAS[4], GEORGE[3], GEORGE[2], SAMUEL[1])* was born 12/08/1900 in Lutherville, Balt. Co. MD, and died 11/1993 in Lutherville. He married HILDA.

Children of Elton Adams and Hilda are:

i. Gladys[7] Adams, b. 11/28/1925.

ii. Bernard Adams, b. 03/17/1926.

iii. Millard Adams, b. 03/12/1927.

iv. Dorothy Adams, b. 06/18/1928.

v. Eunice Adams, b. 03/13/1930.

vi. Robert Adams, b. 04/05/1933.

10. John Carroll[6] Adams *(WILLIAM THOMAS[5], WILLIAM THOMAS[4], GEORGE[3], GEORGE[2], SAMUEL[1])* was born 09/03/1902 in Lutherville, and died 07/09/1990 in Lutherville. He married Margaret.

Child of John Adams and Margaret is:

14. i. Elizbeth Adams[7] Owens, b. 1924.

11. Annabelle[6] Adams *(WILLIAM THOMAS[5], WILLIAM THOMAS[4], GEORGE[3], GEORGE[2], SAMUEL[1])* was born 1905, and died 1928. She married William Brown.

Child of Annabelle Adams and William Brown is:

i. James[7] Brown.

12. Mabel[6] Adams *(WILLIAM THOMAS[5], WILLIAM THOMAS[4], GEORGE[3], GEORGE[2], SAMUEL[1])* was born 1907. She married Calvin Adams, son of Elijah Adams.

Children of Mabel Adams and Calvin Adams are:

i. John[7] Adams.

ii. Rosabelle Adams.

iii. Charles Adams.

13. William Thomas[6] Adams Jr. *(WILLIAM THOMAS[5], WILLIAM THOMAS[4], GEORGE[3], GEORGE[2], SAMUEL[1])* was born 08/25/1908 in Lutherville, MD[21], and died 02/04/1990 in

Lutherville, MD. He married Mary Penny Jenkins 1928 in Lutherville MD.

Children of William Adams and Mary Jenkins are:

15. i. Thomas Charles[7] Adams, b. 08/16/1929, Lutherville, Md.

ii. Mary Adams Cooper, b. 05/11/1931, Lutherville, MD; d. 04/04/1989, Lutherville, MD; m. ALPHONSIS COOPER.

16. iii. William C. S. Adams, b. 05/23/1933, Lutherville, MD.

iv. Sarah Margaret Adams, b. 1935, Lutherville, MD; d. 1939, Lutherville, MD.

17. v. Grace Adams Matthews, b. 02/16/1938, Lutherville, MD.

18. vi. Allen Leroy Adams, b. 02/06/1940.

vii. Kathleen Adams Orem, b. 12/04/1943.

19. viii. Maynard Adams, b. 01/20/1954

APPENDIX

COURT DOCUMENTS

ORDERS BOOK 10
1664-1674 P191

Peter Beckett listed in Titable List in household of John Eyre as

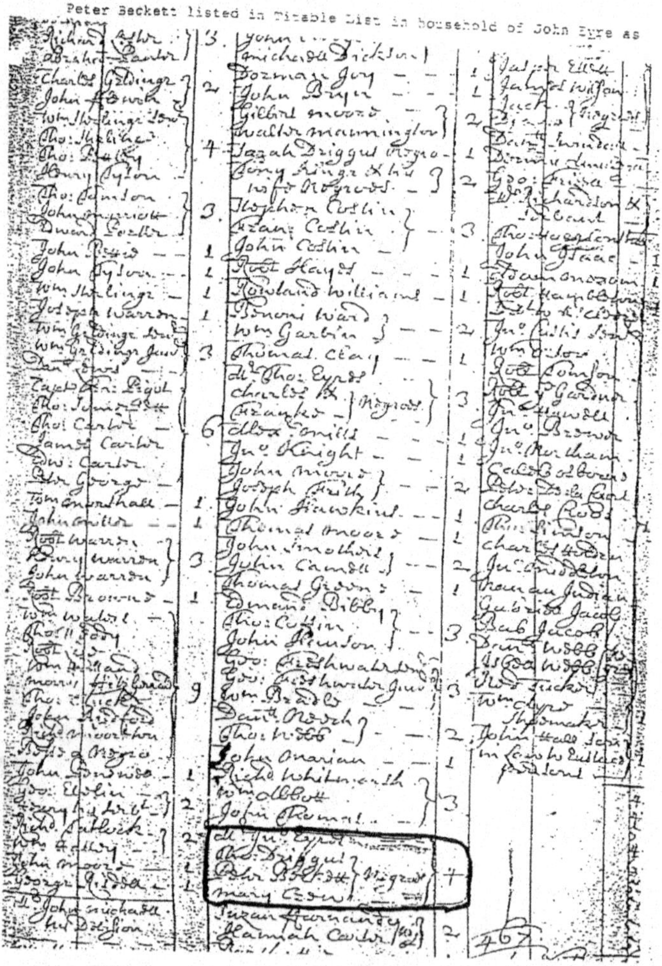

Richard Ashe
Abraham Taylor
Charles Geldinge
John Fenwick
Wm Wellinge Senr
Tho: Wellinge
Tho: Bailey
Henry Tyson
Tho: [illegible]
John Marriott
Edward Foster
John Reed
John Tyson
Wm Wellinge
Joseph Warren
Wm Geldinge Senr
Wm Geldinge Junr
Tho: Carter
James Carter
Edw: Carter
Robt George
Tom Marshall
John Miller
Robt Warren
Henry Warren
John Warren
Robt Browne
Wm Walker
John Goodwin
Richd Bullock
John Moore
George Ridd[illegible]
John Michaell
his [illegible]

Michaell Dickson
Dorman Joy
John Bryer
Gilbert Moore
Walter Mannington
Sarah Driggus Negro
Tony Longo & his wife Negroes
Stephen Costin
Francis Costin
John Costin
Robt Hayes
Rowland Williams
Benoni Ward
Wm Garbin
Thomas Clay
Mr Tho: Eyre
Charles &
Francke } Negroes
Alex Mills
Jno Knight
John Moore
Joseph Bailey
John Hawkins
Thomas Moore
John Smothers
John Camell
Thomas Greene
Edmund Bibby
Tho: Costin
John Henderson
Geo: Freshwater
Geo: Freshwater Junr
Wm Bradly
Danll Roach
Tho: Webb
John Marian
Richd Whitmarsh
Wm Abbott
John Thomas
Mr Jno Eyre
Tho: Driggus
Peter Beckett } Negroes 4
Mary Cowin
Susan Hernandy
Hannah Carter

Ralph Elliott
John Wilson
Jno Richardson & servant
Thos Haggerdon
John Isaac
Edw Anderson
Robt Hayes
Jno Costin Senr
Wm Taylor
Robt Lawson
Robt Gardner
Jno Howell
Jno Browne
Jno Northam
Caleb Osborne
Edw: Dolahead
Charles Rhodes
Thos Simpson
Charles Holden
Jno Middleton
Thomas an Indian
Gabriell Jacob
Bab Jacob
Danll Webb
Isaac Webb
Wm Clyfe
John Hall Senr
467

FREE BORN

List of Tithables 1677

Wm Jarvis 3
Wm Wilson
John Wills
Saint Brander 3
Richd Cole
Bryan Bratton
Richard Cutler 3
[illegible] Carter
Charles Geldinge 2
John Howell
Henry Tylor 4
John Tylor 1
Joseph Warren 1
Wm Geldinge 3
Capt. Fra. Pigot
Tho. Carter
James Carter 6
Wm Carter
Tho. George
Wm Marshall 1
John Miller 1
Robt Warren
Henry Warren 3
John Warren
Robt Browne 1
Tho. Eddy
Morris Hibbard 9
John Andrews 1
Geo. Eldin 2
Richd Aubeck 2

Wm Bros 1
Donham Handum 1
Manuell Driggus 1
Frandll Cossinet
Thomas Ward
Joshua Hitchett 3
John Adolph
Micheall Dickson 2
Dorman Joy 1
John Bryer 1
Gilbert Moore
Walter Manninge 2
Sarah Driggus Negro 1
Tony Kinge & his wife Negroes 2
Stephen Costin
Isaac Costin
John Costin 3
Robt Hayes 1
Rowland Williams 1
Simon Ward
Wm Garbin 2
Thomas Clay 1
Mr Tho. Eyres
Charles &
Franko Negroes 3
Alex Mills 1
Jno Knight 1
John Moore
Joseph [illegible] 2
John Hawkins 1
Thomas Moore 1
John Smothers
John Cande[illegible] 2
Thomas Groome 1
Edmond Bibby
Tho. Coffin
John Renton 3
Geo. Freshwater
Geo. Freshwater Jun
Wm Bradle 3
Danll North
Thos Webb 2
John Marian 1
Richd Whitemarth
Wm Abbott
John Thomas 3
Mr Jno Eyres

John Webb
Henry Pike
Fran Griffith
John Harvey
Jno Stallicome
John Cark
Wm Richardson &
Tho. Hogg
John Isaac
Robt Hampton
Jno Howell
Jno Browne
Jno Northam
Tho. Linton
Charles Holden
Roman Indian
Gabriel Jacob
Rob Jacob
Wm Lynd Shoomaker
John Hall [illegible] in England

FREE BORN

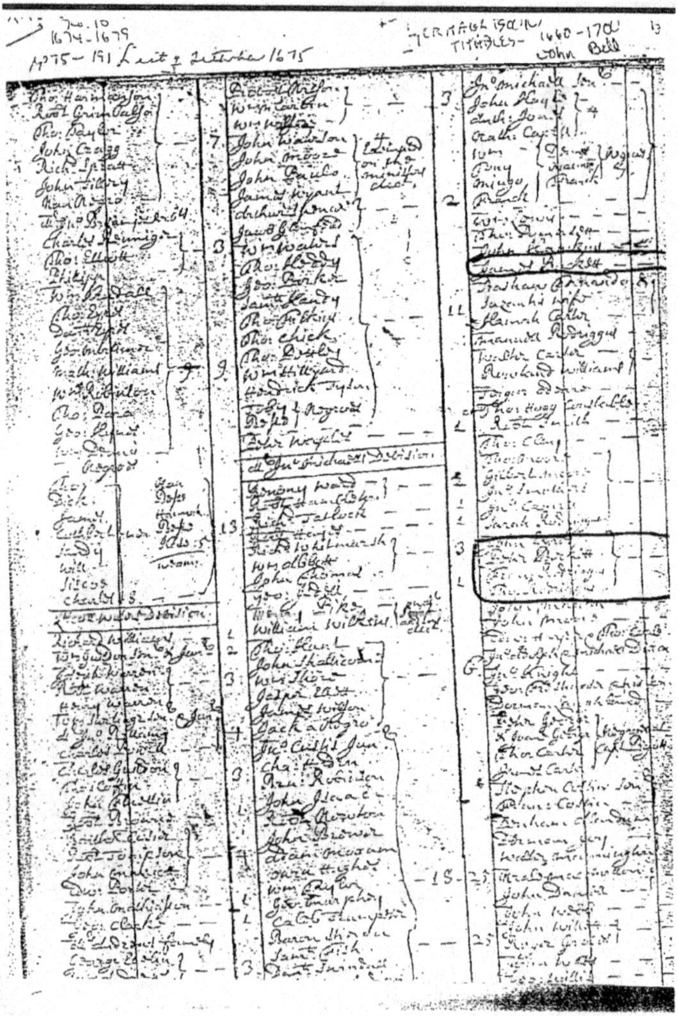

ORDERS, WILLS NO 10
1674-1679 P203

Sarah Dason identured servant to John Eyre adjudged to be age sixteen on November 26, 1677.

"This day John Eyre brought his servant woman named Sarh Dason to the court to have their judgement of her age whom and they adjudged her... sixteen years of age at the ...."

At a Court held in Northampton County the 26th day of November Anno 1677

Lt Coll Wm Waters

Present: Coll Wm Kendall, Major Wm Spencer, Mr John Michaell, Capt Isaac Foxcroft, Capt Fran. Pigot, Mr Argoll Yardley, Mr [illegible], Mr Tho. Harmanson

This day Mr John Eyres brought his servt woman named Sarah Dason to the Court to have their Judgmt of her age whome they adjudged to bee Sixteene yeares of age at the date hereof & to serve according to Act of Assembly.

ORDER BOOK & WILLS 12
1683-1689 P59

Wheras Sarah Dawson servant to Major John Eyre "acknowleges in open court that she hath had three bastard malotto children by her said Master's Negro Slave Peter. It is therefore the judgement of the court and accordingly ordered that after .... for her said offences and that for the loast of the said three offenses the sherriff take her into his cutody and ....forwith ... twenty one lashes on her naked shoulders ..."

Whereas Sarah Dawson servt to Mr Jno Eyre being at last Court to answer to the presentmt made agt her by the Grand Jury for fornication did by her owne Confession acknowledge in open Court that shee hath had three bastard Malotto Children by her said masters Negro Slave Peter. It is therefore the Judgmt of the Court and accordingly ordered that after the time shee came into the Country for bee expired shee serve her said master six yeares according to Act and that for the last of the said three offences the Sheriffe take her into his Custody and see that shee forthwith have twenty one lashes on her Naked Shoulders well laid on as a just reward of her said offence & pay Court charges als execution.

ORDER BOOK & WILLS 12
1683-1689 . P. 442-443

Upon the petition of Sarah the wife of Peter Beckett, slave to Major John Eyre it is the judgment of the court and accordingly ordered that her child is at her own disposal there finding sufficient.. . to hold the parish harmless from the said children as ....skace satusy the said in Eyre for what shall be ....due to him for his charges expanded and trouble of his house about the said child from its birth to the time of her placing it out."
July 1689.

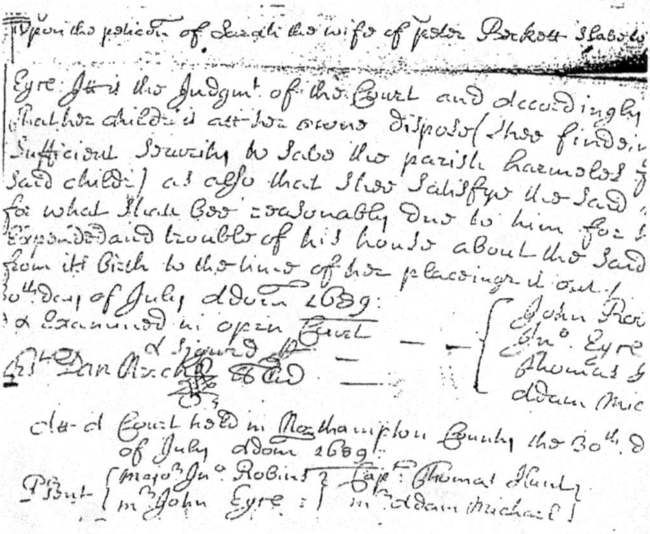
Upon the petition of Sarah the wife of Peter Beckett slave to
Eyre: It is the Judgmt. of the Court and accordingly
that her children is att her owne dispose (shee findin
Sufficient Security to save the parish harmless f
said children) as also that shee satisfye the said
for what shall bee reasonably due to him for
Expended and trouble of his house about the said
from its Birth to the time of her placing it out./
30th Day of July Anno 1689:
& Examined in open Court
& Signed
Test Dan Neech Cl Cur
John Robi
Jno. Eyre
Thomas H
Adam Mic
At a Court held in Northampton County the 30th D
of July Anno 1689
PSent Majr Jno. Robins, Mr John Eyre, Capt Thomas Hunt, Mr Adam Michael

ORDER BOOK & WILLS 14
1698-1710 P. 96

Ann Daughter to Sarah Beckett beinge four yere old tnth of December last with her said mothers consent is this day bound by the court to Mrs. Ann Eyre to serve until eithteene yeares of age accrding to law and to bee at her dispose to which of her children shee shall thinke fitt. The court findeinge noe cause to the contrary before she said girle attained to the age aforesaid.

Ann Daughter to Sarah Beckett Beinge foure yeare old tenth of Dece last (with her said mothers Consent) is this day Bound by the Court to Mrs Ann Eyre to Serve untill Eighteene yeares of Age According to La[w] And to bee at her dispose to which of her children shee shall thinke fi[tt] The Court findeinge Noe cause to the Contrary before the said Girle Attaines to the Age aforesaid.

Page 176

Peter Beckett and Sarah his wife ... suit against John Morrins i[n] an action of Debt this day ...failing to a ... or any attorney for him .... ordered pay... sheriff ... is a case of a ... to th[e] next court.

Peter Beckett and Sarah his wife Compl. suit agst Jno Morrins in an action of Debt for the Deft failing to apear, or any attorney for [illegible] ordered pass agst ye Sheriffe in case of a N. G. [illegible] the next Court

FREE BORN

Order Book No 15
1710-1716 pp 252-253

Ann Beckett received 25 lashes on June 20, 1716 for having a bastard child by John Drighouse

[illegible] Ann Beckett [illegible] by ye Grand Jury [illegible] Ann Beckett [illegible] twenty five lashes well laid on her bare back [illegible]

Order Book No 18
1722-1729 p 394

Gertrude Harmanson came into court...that John Drighouse died without making any will as far as the acknowledgement of the widow of the deceased...

Gertrude Harmanson came into Court & made oath That John Drighouse deced died without making any Will as farr as she knows or believes & the Widow of the deced having in open Court refused to accept of the Adminstr. on the petn. of the said Gertrude Adminstr. is granted her [illegible]

Order Book No 18
1722-1729 p 161

William son of Rebecca bound as apprentice 12 December 1723 to John Robins until he attain the age of twenty one years.

Ordered That William Beckett be bound out to Mr. John Robins untill he attain the age of twenty one years the said William being two years of Age the 12th of December last.

161

A TRUE COPY - TESTE: KENNETH F. ARNOLD, CLERK
BY [signature] DEP. CLERK

Order Book No 20
1732-1742 p 279

Ordered that Peter Beckett aged three years next Febryary be bound apprenticé to Samuel Church and Elizabeth his wife to serve them according to law.

that Peter Becket aged three Years next February be bou
hurch & Elisabeth his Wife to serve them according to Law

Order Book No 21
1742-1748 p 33

he further inventory of the estate of Azarium Drigghouse decesed as presented in court by Mark Becket who intermaried with the decedents widow and executrix is ordered to be recorded.
pond consideration of the petition of Mark Becket who ntermarried with the widow and executrix of Azarium Drigghouse ecd prayin a diviison of the said decedents estated ordered that illiam Burton, William Scott, William Mills and Edw Custis ... r any three of them being first truly sworn do divbide the state of the said Azaricum Drigghouse according to his will and eport the division to the next court.

ther Inventory of the Estate of Azaricum Driggh[ouse] dec'd was
in Court by Mark Becket who Intermarried w.th the s.d Deced[ent]
Executrix w.ch is Ordered to be Recorded.

sideration of the Petition of Mark Becket who intermarried w
& Executrix of Azaricum Driggh[ouse] dec'd praying a Divisi
Decedents Estate Ordered that William Burton, William Scott
Mills & Edm.d Custis Gent.s or any three of them being first sw
Divide the Estate of the said Azaricum Driggh[ouse] according
& report the Division to the next Court.

Order Book No 21
1742-1748 p344

Ordered that the curchwardens of Hungars Parish do bind Rachell the daughter of Sarah BEcket unto Posthumus Core according to Sam the said Rachell being three years of age the twenty fifth day of May last.

Ordered that the Churchwardens of Hungars Parish do bind Rachell the daughter of Sarah Becket unto Posthumus Core according to Sam, the said Rachell being three years of age the Twenty fifth Day of May last

Court Orders No 22
1748-1751 p 3

Ordered that the churchwardens of Hungars Parish do bind Leah Becket orphan aged nine years the last day of August next unto Richard Hanby according to Law.

Ordered that the Churchwardens of Hungars Parish do bind Leah Beck Orphan aged nine years the last Day of August next unto Richar according to Law.

Court Orders No 22
1748-1751 p 130

Ordered that the Churchwardens of Hungars Parish do bind ...William Becket Orphan Negro aged seven years the sixth day of last August unto Elenor Ellegood according to Law.

FREE BORN

Court Orders No 22
1748-1751 p 139-40

On the petition of Sarah Becket Negro it is ordered, that her son Spencer be bound by the Churchwardens of Hungars Parish unto William Bradford according to Law the said orphan being one year of age the seventeeth day of October next week.

in the Petition of Sarah Becket Negro, It is Ordered that her
son Spencer be bound by the Churchwardens of Hungars Parish
unto

Order Book No 24
1753-1758 p 477

Ordered that the Churchwardens do bind Comfort Becket Negro orphan aged four years last December to Caleb Scott according to Law.

Ordered that the Churchwardens do bind Comfort Becket Negro Orphan aged four
last December to Caleb Scott according to Law.

Minute Book 25
1754-61 p 205

Ordered that John Becket neg son of Sarah Becket be bound to Zerobell Downing according to law, being 3 year old last September

Ord. that John Becket neg. Son of Sarah Becket be bound
to Zorobabell Downing acc. to Law being 3 year old last Sept.

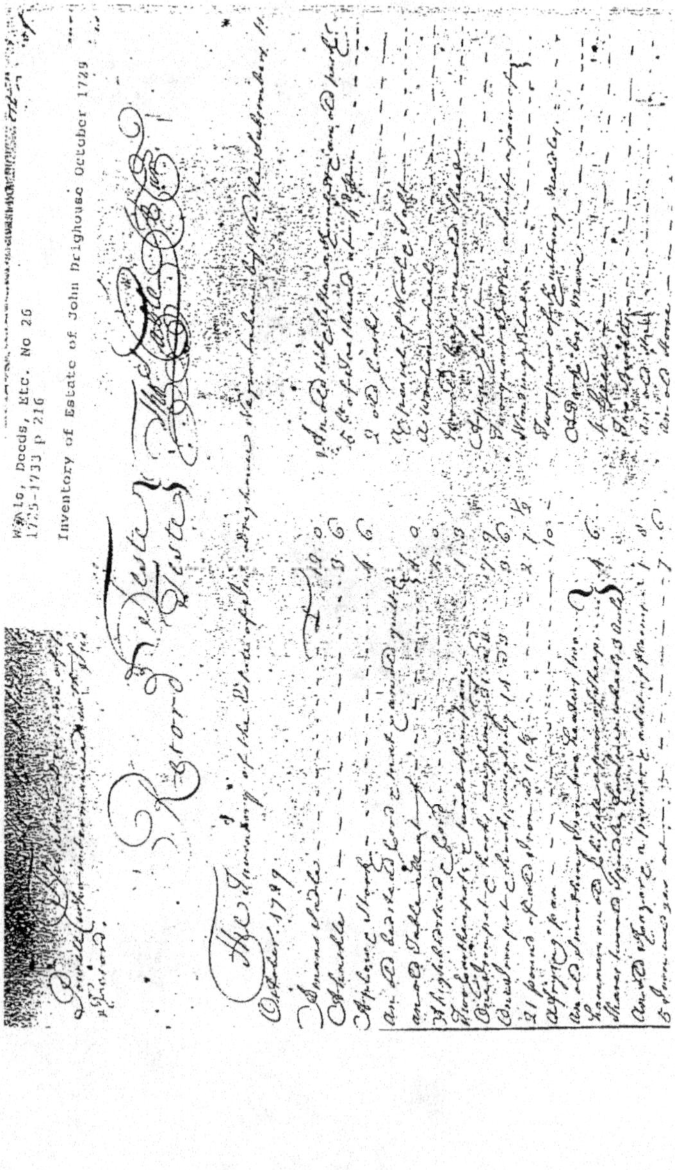
Wills, Deeds, Etc. No 26
1725-1733 p 216

Inventory of Estate of John Brighouse October 1729

& Inventories No 21
1754-1760 p 281

Thomas Drighouse free Negro last will and testatment bequething possessions to Jane Becket and her daughters Betty, Lydia and Hester and appointing Jane exectrix.

In the name of God Amen, I Thomas Drighouse of the County of Northampton free Negro, do by these Presents make this my last Will and Testament in manner and form following. Imprimis I give and Bequeath to Jane Becket one Bed and furniture during her life, and after her Death to return to her Daughter Betty to her and her Heirs forever. Item I give and Bequeath to Jane Beckets Daughters Betty and Lydia three Beds & their furnitures, to be equally Divided to them & their Heirs forever. Item I give and Bequeath to Jane Becket, one Mare named Dapple to her and her Heirs forever. Item I give and Bequeath to Jane Beck Daughters Betty & Lydia, each of them three Cows to them & their Heirs forever. Item I give and Bequeath to Jane Beckets Daughters Betty and Lydia each of them a Pewter Dish and Plate to them and their Heirs forever. Item I give an Bequeath to Jane Becket & to her Daughters Hester and Betty and Lydia, all my Sheep to be equally Divided to them and their Heirs forever. Item I give and

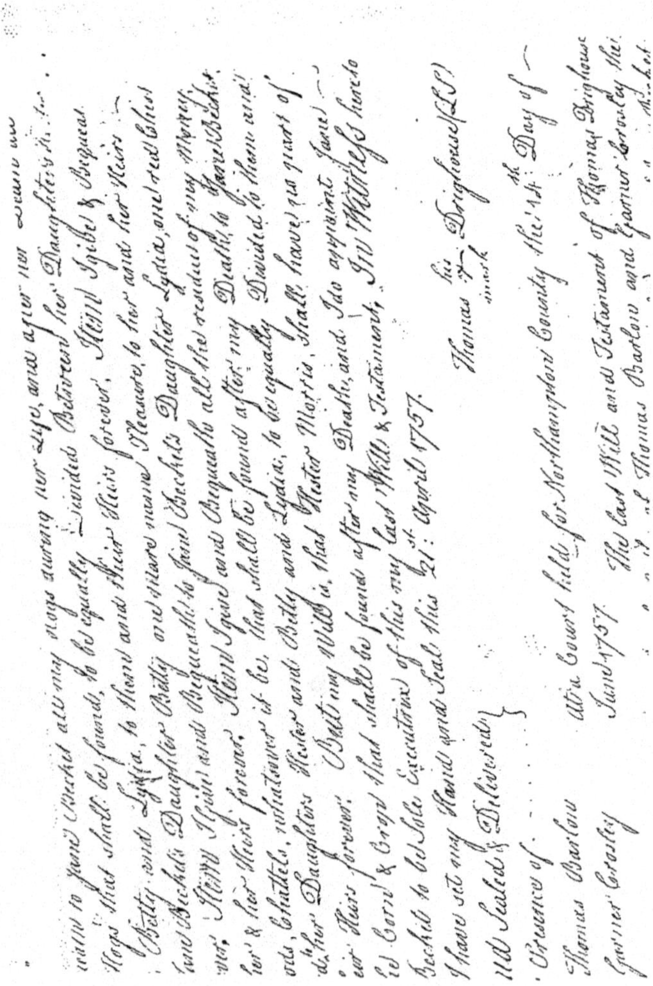

...eath to Jane Becket all my Hogs during her Life, and after her Death all
Hogs that shall be found, to be equally Divided Between her Daughters H...
Betty and Lydia, to them and their Heirs forever. Item I give & Bequeat...
Jane Becket's Daughter Betty one Mare name Pleasure, to her and her Heirs
...ever. Item I give and Bequeath to Jane Becket's Daughter Lydia, one red Ches...
her & her Heirs forever. Item I give and Bequeath all the residue of my Money,
...ods, Chattels, whatsoever it be, that shall be found after my Death, to Jane Becket,
...d her Daughters Hester and Betty and Lydia, to be equally Divided to them and
...eir Heirs forever. But my Will is, that Hester Morris, shall have no part of
...ed Corn & Crop that shall be found after my Death, and I do appoint Jane
Beckit to be Sole Executrix of this my last Will & Testament, In Witness hereto
I have set my Hand and Seal this 21st April 1757.

Thomas his + mark Brighouse (LS)

...ed Sealed & Delivered } in Presence of
Thomas Barlow
Garner Crosley

At a Court held for Northampton County the 14th Day of June 1757.
The last Will and Testament of Thomas Brighouse ... Thomas Barlow and Garner Crosley the...

FREE BORN

Certificates of Freedom from Caroline County Records

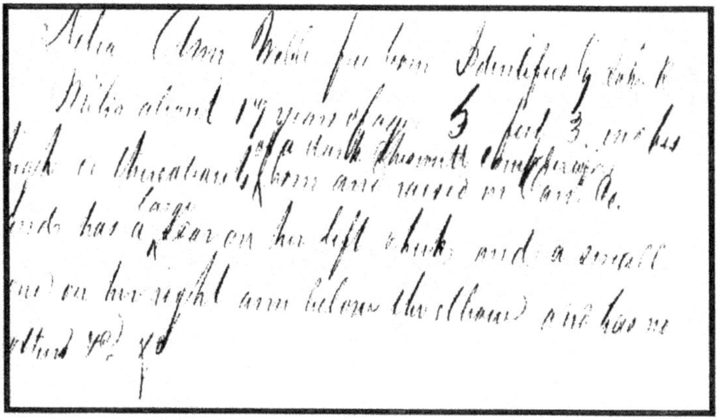
[illegible] Ann Willis free born Identified by John R. Willis about 17 years of age 5 feet 3 inches high or thereabouts of a dark chestnut complexion born and raised in Car. Co. [illegible] has a large scar on her left cheek and a small one on her right arm below the elbow and has no [illegible]

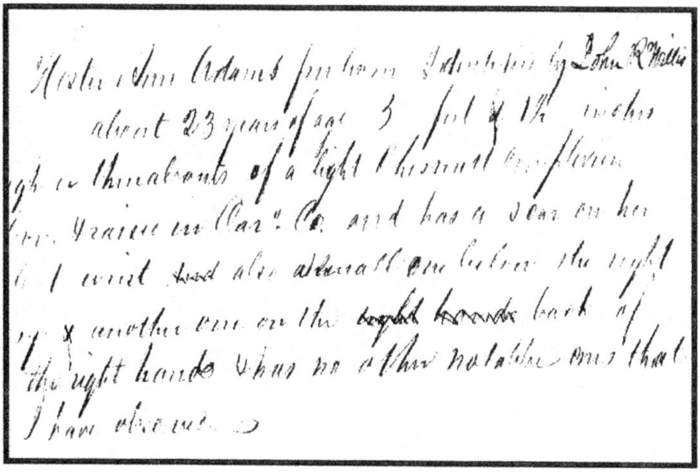
Hester Ann Adams free born Identified by John R. Willis about 23 years of age 5 feet 1½ inches high or thereabouts of a light chestnut complexion born & raised in Car. Co. and has a scar on her [illegible] wrist and also a small one below the right [illegible] another one on the ~~right hand~~ back of the right hand & has no other notable ones that I have observed

FREE BORN

Certificates of Freedom from Caroline County Records

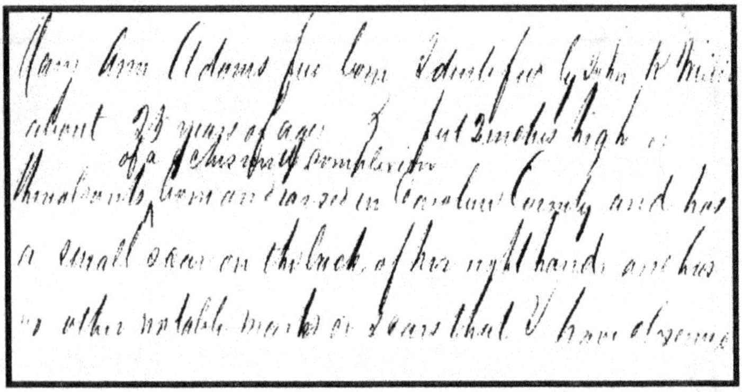
Mary Ann Adams free born Identified by John R Willi[s] about 23 years of age 5 feet 2 inches high or thereabouts of a chestnut complexion born and raised in Caroline County and has a small scar on the back of her right hand and has no other notable marks or scars that I have discerned

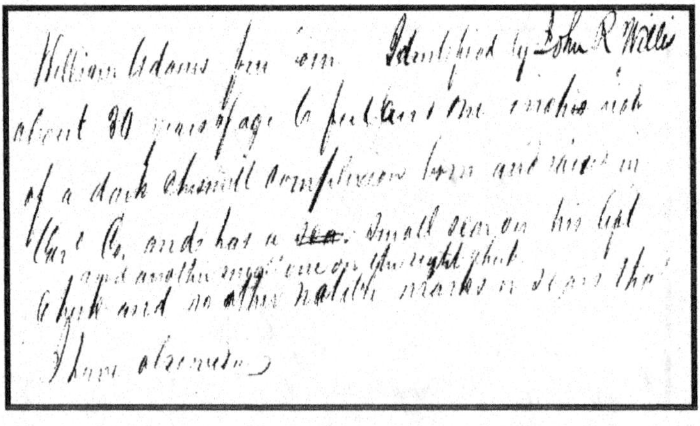
William Adams free born Identified by John R Willi[s] about 30 years of age 6 feet and one inches high of a dark chestnut complexion born and raised in Car. Co. and has a ~~sca~~ small scar on his left cheek and another one on the right cheek and no other notable marks or scars that I have discerned

INDEX

ENDNOTES

---

[1] Heinegg, Paul, Free African Americans of North Carolina and Virginia, Clearfield Publishing, Baltimore, MD, 1994, p 79ff.

[2] Coldham, Peter, Emigrants in Chains, Genealogical Publishing CO, Surrey, England, 1994, p 5.

[3] Coldham, p. 99.

[4] McKey, JoAnn, Accomack County Virginia Court Order Abstracts 1663-1666, Heritage Books, Bowie, MD. p viii.

[5] McKey,p 144.

[6] McKey, p.60.

[7] Coldham, p. 131.

[8] Breen and Innes, Myne Owne Grounde, Oxford University Press, New York, N.Y., 1970, p.. 44.

[9] Ibid.

[10] Ibid.. P. 70 ff.

[11] Deal, J. Douglas, Race and Class in Colonial Virginia, Garland Publishers, New York, 1993, p. 178ff.

[12] Johnson, James, Race Relations in Virginia and Miscegenation in the South, U of Mass Press, Amherst, 1970, pp 177-81.

[13] Deal, p. 180.

[14] Breen and Innes, p 86 ff.

[15] Ibid., p. 87.

[16] Cavliers and Pioneers, p.290

[17] Bell,John. Northhampton County, Virginia, Tithables , 1662-1677, pp.20ff.

[18] Bell, John. Northhampton County, Virginia, Tithables, 1720-1769. Heritage Books, Bowie, Md, p. vi.

[19] Bell, John. Northhampton County, Virginia, Tithables , 1662-1677. p 58.

[20] Wise, Jennings, Ye Kingdome of Accowmacke, Bell Book and Stationery, p. 363.

[21] Whitelaw, Ralph, Virginia's Eastern Shore, Virginia Historical Society, p. 64.

[22] Ibid.

[23] Deal., p. 35.

[24] Northampton County Orders 1664-74 p. 114.

[25] Northampton County Orders 1674-79, pp 75,191,203.

[26] Coldham, Peter Wilson, Bristol Registers of Servants to Foreign Plantations, Genealogical Publishing, 1988, p. 317.

[27] Northampton County Orders and Wills, 1674-1679, p.203.

[28] Northampton County Orders & Wills 1683-89, p.59

[29] Northampton County Orders and Wills , 1683-1689 p. 442.

[30] Northampton County Orders and Wills 1664-74, f. 52.

[31] Northampton County Orders and Wills, 1664-74, f. 122.

[32] Northampton County Orders and Wills 1698-1710, p.96

[33] Northampton County Orders and Wills 1710-16, p.252

[34] Northampton County Orders and Wills 21:281

[35] Northampton County Orders and Wills 1742-8, pI.33

[36] Northampton County Orders and Wills 1640-5, p.457.

[37] Northampton County Orders and Wills 1645-51, p. 20

[38] Northampton County Orders and Wills 1651-4,p. 114.

[39] Virginia Genealogist v 17 no 4 pp 259-60.

[40] Northampton County Orders and Wills 1722-29 p. 394

[41] Northampton County Orders and Wills 1698-1710 p. 96.

[42] Northampton County Orders and Wills 1732-42 p. 279.

[43] Northampton County Orders and Wills 1748-51 p. 130.

[44] Northampton County Orders and Wills 18:161

[45] Northampton County Orders and Wills 1783-1787.

[46] Northampton County Orders and Wills 1748-51 p. 3.

[47] Northampton County Orders and Wills 1742-48 p. 344.

[48] Northampton County Orders and Wills 1758-61 p. 129.

[49] Northampton County Minutes 1765-71 p. 46.

[50] Northampton County Orders and Wills 1753-8 p. 477.

[51] Minutes 1765-71 p. 46.

[52] Minutes 1765-71 p. 46.

[53] Guild, Jane Purcell, Black Codes of Virginia, Willow Bend Books, 1995.

[54] Northampton County Orders and Wills, 1698-1710 p.96

[55] Northampton County Orders and Wills 1710-16 p. 252

[56] Northampton County Orders and Wills 1742-8, pp.33, 56

[57] Northampton County Orders and Wills 1783-87, p. 379.

[58] Northampton County Orders and Wills 1722-29 p. 394

[59] Northampton County Orders and Wills 1732-42 p.130.

[60] Northampton County Orders and Wills 1748-51, p. 130.

[61] Northampton County Orders and Wills 18: 161

[62] Northampton County Orders and Wills LP 35

[63] Northampton County Orders and Wills 1738-51, p.3

[64] Northampton County Orders and Wills 1742-48, p 344

[65] The Census of Virginia. P.82.

[66] Ibid.

[67] Tylers Quarterly, v.2, No.3, p. 129.

[68] Northampton County Orders and Wills 1832-6, p. 251.

[69] Northampton County Orders and Wills 1832-6, p. 251

[70] 1850 Accomack County Census

[71] 1860 Accomack County Census

[72] Wright, James, The Free Negro in Maryland, Octogon Books, New York, 1971, p.94ff

www.ingramcontent.com/pod-product-compliance
Lightning Source LLC
Chambersburg PA
CBHW070804290326
41931CB00011BA/2130
* 9 7 8 0 7 8 8 4 1 6 2 5 5 *